THE CHAMBER

Greater Kansas City Chamber of Commerce

Kansas City

▨ A PORTRAIT OF PROGRESS ▨

Corporate Profiles by Sally Pfeffer • Featuring photography of MIDWESTOCK

The Greater Kansas City Chamber of Commerce and Community Communications, Inc.

would like to express our gratitude to the following companies for their leadership in the development of this book.

UTILICORP UNITED

Kansas City

A PORTRAIT OF PROGRESS

Corporate Profiles by Sally Pfeffer • Featuring photography of MIDWESTOCK

Kansas City

⊡ A PORTRAIT OF PROGRESS ⊡

Corporate Profiles by Sally Pfeffer

Photos provided by MIDWESTOCK

Produced in cooperation with the Greater Kansas City Chamber of Commerce

Ronald P. Beers, Publisher

Staff for *Kansas City: A Portrait of Progress*

Acquisitions	**Henry S. Beers**
Publisher's Sales Associate	**Elizabeth Kibbodeaux**
Editor in Chief	**Wendi L. Lewis**
Profile Editors	**Amanda J. Burbank and Christi Stevens**
Design Director	**Scott Phillips**
Designers	**Matt Johnson and Christi Scruggs**
Photo Editors	**Wendi L. Lewis and Matt Johnson**
Production Manager	**Christi Stevens**
Accounting Services	**Stephanie Perez**
Pre-Press and Separations	**Classic Printing**
Printing Production	**Walsworth Printing**

CCI

Community Communications, Inc.

Montgomery, Alabama

David M. Williamson, Chief Executive Officer

Ronald P. Beers, President

W. David Brown, Chief Operating Officer

Cover image © Kevin Sink, MIDWESTOCK

The fall season brings a mellow rainbow of oranges, browns, and yellows to the leaves of sugar and silver maple trees. © Charles Gurche, MIDWESTOCK

Following page: © Kevin Sink, MIDWESTOCK

Foreword

From the confluence of the Kaw and Missouri Rivers, to a vibrant bistate community encompassing 11 counties...

From the trading post of a French fur trapper, to the home of 1.7-million people...

Welcome to *Kansas City: A Portrait of Progress*.

Explore the pages of this book, and you'll begin to understand the affection in which we hold our community.

Inside, you'll be able to stroll the boulevards, admire one of our many fountains, and see the smiles of our children. Greater Kansas City is a community of strong neighborhoods, made up of lush green suburbs, brick fourplexes, renovated loft space, and lakeside developments. It has been home to a President, Walt Disney, Jesse James, and Walter Cronkite; its history shaped by political bosses, bridges, and beef-on-the-hoof.

Yesterday's stockyards are gone, but Greater Kansas City's railroads are still humming through a bistate region boasting a vibrant business community. Cultural offerings range from Bach to Basie, Shakespeare to Simon, ballet, opera, and art. Appetites can be satisfied from barbecue to bean curd, Mongolian to Mandarin, family style to formal. You can tailgate at a Chiefs game or cheer on your kid's soccer team. Greater Kansas City offers a quality of life that surprises newcomers and is sometimes taken for granted by the rest of us.

The Chamber is pleased to bring you this book. It reminds us of who we are: diverse but connected. Many cities—but one community.

Peter S. Levi, President
Greater Kansas City Chamber of Commerce

The massive sculptures on the top of Bartle Hall were constructed in 1994 and created a dramatic addition to the Kansas City skyline. The sculptures, "Sky Stations/Pylon Caps," are lighted at night and can be seen for several miles. The sculptures' Art Deco style reflects the architecture of the adjacent 1930s-era buildings. © Kevin Sink, MIDWESTOCK

Part One

Chapter One

A COOPERATIVE SPIRIT

First-time visitors to Kansas City are always surprised to find a beautiful, rich, diverse, and sophisticated city. Notions of a flat, arid town in the middle of the American Prairie vanish when they discover an upbeat metropolis populated by levelheaded, hardworking citizens with extraordinarily generous spirits, a commitment to values, a desire to achieve, and love for their community. Newcomers discover what so many others have before them, that the heart of America has a generous heart.

Metropolitan Kansas City is a diverse, textured community built by people who mostly were headed somewhere else and were stopped in their tracks by the beauty and opportunity of this place. French fur traders built a settlement along the Missouri riverfront in 1820, where they bartered with the indigenous peoples who hunted and farmed near the confluence of the Missouri and Kansas rivers. In 1821, William Becknell set out from Independence, Missouri, to Santa Fe and returned with saddlebags bulging with silver. The Santa Fe Trail quickly became a bustling international trade route carrying thousands of commercial, military, and pioneer emigrant wagons. It put the Kansas City region on the map as the "Gateway to the West."

Not everyone heard the call to "Go West." Many travelers opted to put down roots once they arrived here at the start of what became the Sante Fe, Oregon, and California Trails. Here, they farmed fertile upland meadows and built small communities to share the work of the frontier.

These little communities along the trails prospered: Independence, Westport Landing, Merriam, Olathe, and others. On the Missouri riverfront, as its population grew, the small rag-tag community agreed to incorporate in 1850 as the Town of Kansas. Citizens formally adopted the name Kansas City in 1853, but many residents chose to call it "Gully Town" because of the rutted roads blasted through the limestone bluffs south of the River.

Across the river, hundreds of people poured into the Kansas Territory to lay squatters' claims or snatch up $500 shares of newly formed town companies. People arrived from the East and from the South, bringing differing ideas about slavery and states' rights. Sentiments over freedom ran so deep they bitterly divided the community, neighbors against neighbors, family members against kin. With Missouri in the Confederacy and Kansas entering the Union as a Free State, Kansas City

(Right) Union Station on Opening Day, 1914.

(Opposite) Built in 1914, Union Station served as an important link in cross-continental travel during the glory days of rail traffic. At one time, more than 75,000 trains per year stopped at Union Station. Today, North America's second largest train station is now home to Science City, restaurants, and shops.

Photo Courtesy Chris Wilborn & Associates

(Above left) Dedicated in 1995, the Children's Fountain at 32nd Street and North Oak Trafficway is sometimes called the "fountain of youth." The work of Kansas City artist Tom Corbin, it features bronze sculptures of six children frolicking in a giant water basin. The fountain runs in the winter, creating dramatic ice sculptures.

(Right) Kansas City, Kansas, is home to more than 157,900 citizens.

found itself not on the edge but at the very center of the War Between the States.

Even though the Civil War decimated the population and devastated the economy, Kansas Citians didn't give up on themselves or their community. The challenge of recovery became economic opportunity. Civic boosters invited railroads to town and successfully lobbied Congress for funds to build the Hannibal Bridge in 1869, the first to span the Missouri River. With the trains came industry, jobs, and workers. In the next twenty years, Kansas City grew more rapidly than any city west of the Mississippi—from four thousand souls in 1865 to sixty-five thousand in 1880.

Towns sprang up all along the railroad lines: Rosedale, Argentine, Holliday, Stilwell, Morris, Lee's Summit, and more. Roads fostered the new communities. Once part of the "California Road," the street known today as Shawnee Mission Parkway was the forerunner of concepts such as the College Boulevard corridor because it was a roadway that attracted residents, merchants, professional businesses, and faith groups—what today is called "mixed use."

Making a living here took hard work, courage, quick thinking, and ingenuity, characteristics still found in

today's Kansas Citians. The most successful of these early residents dedicated themselves to more than just getting by—they set about improving the quality of life in Kansas City. In 1887, civic leaders formed the Commercial Club, a forerunner of the Greater Kansas City Chamber of Commerce. They called on their fellow citizens "to make Kansas City a good place to live." They campaigned for lighted streets, pavement to cover muddy roads, and sidewalks to replace old boards in front of businesses. They built boulevards, developed parks, placed fountains, and formed neighborhoods that still exist today.

From its beginning, Kansas City has drawn strength and vitality from a fascinating blend of its citizens' customs, histories, economies, and politics. Diversity, in fact, defines metropolitan residents. They came from around the world, originally to work, farm, evangelize, or escape persecution: French, Italian, African-American, Scandinavian, Mexican, Irish, Greek, German, Russian, Armenian, Czech, Serb, Bohemian, and Pole. They joined native-born Americans of British descent who also made the journey west. They were Catholics, Jews, Protestants, Muslims, and many different faiths.

They formed neighborhoods with others who shared their language, religious beliefs, and customs. In recent

© Kevin Sink, MIDWESTOCK

(Left) The Broadway Bridge is one of 13 bridges spanning the Missouri River.

(Following page) A statue of Westport's earliest contributors is found in Pioneer Park at the corner of Westport Road and Broadway. The park features an in-ground map of the United States during the time of westward expansion, complete with pioneer and explorer routes marked so history buffs can trace the early trails.

years, the mix of new residents has added to the veritable kaleidoscope of cultures throughout the region. Communities of Hispanics, Pakistanis, Vietnamese, and other nationalities are woven into the fiber of civic life, adding even more variety, energy, and potency. This is why Kansas City works and works better than most other places.

Diversity also buoys the Kansas City economy, buffering the business sector from many of the nation's economic stumbles and tumbles. Service jobs, from the professions of law, medicine, and finance to hands-on service such as hospitality and barbering, provide the most income for area residents. But, the community at large is also robust in manufacturing, transportation, insurance, wholesale and retail sales, and a wide variety of government activities from the federal level to the township.

Even the region's topography is diverse: Rolling hills and massive limestone bluffs touch broad fertile

grasslands. Rivers, streams, and creeks ribbon the valleys. Sunrise gilds the tops of more than three hundred varieties of trees. Bright noon sunlight glistens off high-rise windows. And, finally, at day's end, inimitable sunsets sweep the broad horizon with breathtaking strokes of orange, magenta, and indigo light. Even the weather is some of everything—snowy winters, scented springs, sizzling summers, and absolutely gorgeous autumns. No one lives here long without realizing that the seasons can change rapidly, often rushing from summer into fall between lunch and supper.

Kansas City has learned how to capitalize on its diversity, using it to help rather than hinder, to support rather than separate its people. In the late 1990s, thousands of civic and business leaders identified six hundred actions to transform Kansas City, Missouri, into the New American City of the 21st Century. They believed the personal qualities that made Kansas City a great city in

© Kevin Sink, MIDWESTOCK

Shawnee Indian Mission State Historic Site offers exhibits on the Methodist missionaries who established the first Shawnee Methodist Mission, and the children they taught. The missionaries were led by Reverend Thomas Johnson, appointed missionary to the Shawnees, and his brother William, missionary to the Kansa tribe. Visitors can tour the residences where the students lived and learned, and portions of what would have been the Johnson family living quarters. The east building serves as the main museum and contains exhibits dealing with a variety of manual trades taught at the mission such as blacksmithing, weaving, and sewing. Shawnee Indian Mission provides a number of educational programs and activities for all ages.

© Bruce Mathews, MIDWESTOCK

"The Kansas City Spirit increasingly transcends governmental boundaries. Throughout the metropolitan area people have joined together for many worthwhile causes such as United Way, support of the arts, economic development, and the unprecedented passage of a bi-state sales tax to restore historic Union Station. Butler Manufacturing Company made Kansas City its home 100 years ago, and its associates represent the Kansas City Spirit. While living throughout the metropolitan area, they are proud to call Kansas City their home."

Donald H. Pratt
Chairman of the Board
Butler Manufacturing Company

(Left) Harry S. Truman was the 33rd President of the United States. Truman moved several times in his childhood and youth— first in 1887 to a farm near Grandview, Missouri; then in 1890 to Independence, Missouri; and finally in 1902 to Kansas City. After he left the White House he and his wife, Bess, returned to Independence.

In the 1950s, Joyce Hall, the founder of Hallmark Cards, conceived the idea of an urban renewal project known today as Crown Center. The dramatic pool fountain, a popular attraction at Crown Center, has no visible retaining basin, plumbing, or nozzles. Forty-nine water jets coupled with bright colored lights are placed under a special grating.

the first place—a willingness to take a bold step, a drive to rebuild after disaster strikes, the old-fashioned Midwestern sensibility and civility—will move the city forward. The result was FOCUS (Forging Our Comprehensive Urban Strategies), the City of Kansas City, Missouri, Master plan. FOCUS emphasizes connection—people with places, with one another, with their heritage, and with their future.

FOCUS concentrated on Kansas City, Missouri. But its goal is shared metro-wide: *Act with a unified strategy to build a community that works for its people.* The historic formation of the Unified Government of Wyandotte County, continuing governing structure for the county and Kansas City, Kansas, illustrated how leaders could yield their turf for the common welfare. The creation of the Bistate Cultural District in the 1990s also demonstrated this principle. People with diverse interests came

together to work for the community at large. Historic legislation created a Bistate Cultural Tax District for shared projects, and generated funds to remodel the historic Union Station and develop Science City as a regional attraction.

The best aspects of this community—exemplified in arts and culture, sports, neighborhoods, faith, education, commerce, and philanthropy—all belong to the cooperative spirit within the people of Greater Kansas City. Through World Wars, destructive floods and fires, the Great Depression, and other catastrophic events, Kansas City always offered its people another chance if they worked together. And work together they have to form community, to overcome adversity, to speak with one voice in support of common goals. ▨

Kansas City, Missouri is known as the "City of Fountains"

Local growers sell their wares throughout the early summer at one of several farmers' markets, such as this one in downtown Overland Park, Kansas.

© Bruce Mathews, MIDWESTOCK

There are many indoor and outdoor activities available for seniors throughout Kansas City.

The Country Club Plaza is Kansas City's most charming shopping, dining, and entertainment district, with 180 unique shops and restaurants.

(Above) Inspired by the late civic and community leader Bruce R. Watkins, the Spirit of Freedom Fountain honors the contributions of Kansas City's African-American residents.

(Left) The Liberty Memorial is the largest monument in the country dedicated to those who served in World War I.

2

Chapter Two

GOOD NEIGHBORS

**The rich variety of Kansas City's neighborhoods inspires
the preservation and sharing of cultures and traditions.**

© Kevin Sink, MIDWESTOCK

There are places in Kansas City where neighbors meet at the fence to share the joys and concerns of their everyday lives. They sit on front stoops and wave to passers-by. Grown-ups line the streets to watch with pride as their children march by in a parade. Couples gather for good conversation and great food in backyards. There are places where friends carry steaming covered dishes to a family faced with crisis, and where church ladies sew quilts to give to newborns in their congregation. There are places where teachers in classrooms ignite imaginations, and where mentors in offices encourage dreams of achievement.

These are only some of the special places in the hundreds of neighborhoods that are the building blocks of Greater Kansas City. Neighborhoods of people who set a standard for livability envied by most large cities. Neighborhoods of people who care about their families, their friends, and their community. Neighborhoods of people who share values and interests and eventually share the experiences that come from living side by side.

In Kansas City's neighborhoods, people understand that making a community requires more than governance or infrastructure. It means simple acts such as planting flowers, picking up trash, and putting a fresh coat of paint on the front of a building. It means voting and attending meetings at city hall. Or baking brownies for the teachers' lounge and volunteering to listen to a second grader read *Ramona Forever*. It means knowing what the neighborhood was like years ago, taking part in what it has become today, and caring about what it can be in the future.

Kansas City is a mosaic of neighborhoods covering two states, 11 counties, and 136 communities. Kansas City, Missouri, alone has more than 300 unique and distinct neighborhoods, each with its own flavor and charm, architecture and history. Many neighborhoods are historic, with names like Columbus Park and Hyde Park, Union Hill and Quality Hill, Briarcliff and Brookside, Santa Fe Place and Janssen Place. Encircling Kansas City, Missouri, are hundreds of other significant neighborhoods—many of them cities in their own right. From Strawberry Hill to Lake Winnebago, Weatherby

© Jeff Morgan, MIDWESTOCK

Developer J.C. Nichols knew that neighborhoods were more than real estate. He placed sculptures and quiet fountains within expansive green spaces of Crestwood, Brookside, Armour Hills, along Ward Parkway, and in Fairway, Prairie Village, and Mission Hills.

Lake to Stilwell, every compass point and in between is defined by neighborhoods.

Points across the world map are well represented in Kansas City, a wonderful and unexpected blending of people and places over a period of nearly two hundred years. They came to farm, work in steel mills, meat packaging plants, and construction. At times in the late nineteenth and early twentieth centuries, they arrived in such great numbers that houses could not be built fast enough and many simply lived in tents. But, they kept coming and kept building, soon stretching the confines of early settlements in every direction, building newer homes and businesses, forming neighborhoods north and south of the Missouri River and east and west of state line. By the late twentieth century,

Residential choices include suburban neighborhoods, multi-family dwellings, historic homes and neighborhoods, and renovated, revitalized buildings in the heart of the city. These cheerful flower boxes add a homey warmth to the choice of an urban residence.

needs. Sidewalks need improvement? Need help with loans to fix up housing? Need to attract new homeowners to their street? People threw block parties and formed homes association and got to know each other. They defined fundamentals of neighborhood identity: conservation of historic assets to maintain the character of the neighborhood, code enforcement to improve housing conditions, and design standards for new housing that capitalize on the characteristics of the area.

As a result, many people in urban Kansas City are reinvesting and reinventing neighborhoods. Attractive, affordable new homes in reclaimed areas; restaurants and amenities in the historic 18th & Vine Historic Jazz District; new loft apartments in the River Market. These new homes and new business are drawing people back to the urban core, to planned "urban villages" where residents can be within walking distance of daily things they need, cultural attractions, and even their work.

The Livable Neighborhoods Task Force has similar goals and results in Kansas City, Kansas. Individual KCK homes associations, such as the Historic Westheight Neighborhood Association, also work to preserve the special character of the housing stock in their locale. In fact, all over the region, city leaders and citizen groups are actively preserving historic town squares and downtowns, updating older residential areas with better street lighting, new parks and sidewalks, and helping new development harmonize with existing structures.

The area's regional planning organization, the Mid-America Regional Council (MARC), recently undertook a community-building initiative, Creating Quality Places, that produced a set of twenty design principles to guide development while preserving and enhancing the quality of life for all residents. The Creating Quality Places initiative showed that residents throughout the Kansas City region want neighborhoods that offer choices in housing types and sizes, that meet the needs of different economic groups and age levels, that provide residents with a sense of identity and encourage continuous renewal and reinvestment.

Another MARC community-wide effort, Metro Outlook, reviewed hundreds of statistics and opinions about the Kansas City area to evaluate the quality of life, detect trends and challenges, and to spur discussions among leaders about vital changes needed to make Kansas City an even better place to live. Researchers found the sense of community runs strong in metropolitan Kansas City. Citizens care deeply about their quality of life and they want to live in a place where that quality is improving for everyone. They want safe neighborhoods, good health, and strong families, but they also want their leaders to address challenging shared issues, such as education, racial diversity, health care costs, and affordable housing.

technology and life sciences were encouraging another new influx of talented people to come to the area.

The sense of community in Kansas City comes from a deliberate design on the part of city leaders and neighborhood associations to come together to make their corner of the world a better place to live. Many area cities have undertaken master plans in the past ten years, and they are sharing the plans with each other to increase the potential of the metropolitan area as a whole.

One of the most important lessons learned from the FOCUS (Forging Our Comprehensive Urban Strategy) process was the desirability of improving neighborhoods by connecting people with others within their neighborhoods and then connecting the neighborhoods to city hall. Neighbors who barely knew one another came together for meetings to learn how to evaluate their

A renovated and redeveloped historic district adjacent to Kansas City's Central business district, Quality Hill was created through an innovative partnership between a private developer, the city, and twenty local companies, including the Hall Family Foundation. Together, this group invested $4 million, establishing initial momentum for the improvement of key blocks, and eventually leading to major reinvestment in the area.

© Bruce Mathews, MIDWESTOCK

Metro Outlook will evaluate Kansas City on an on-going basis to enhance the region's ability to work together to find solutions for problems, new talent and resources, and retain educated, creative workers.

Given the historic Kansas City spirit—defined by legendary former City Manager L.P. Cookingham as "a willingness on the part of the people to participate in civic improvement"—Kansas Citians will indeed rise to this challenge. Whether they live in the urban core or the suburbs, in a loft condominium or a lake house, in a split-level home or a high-rise apartment, in a mansion or a mobile home, Kansas Citians are coming together as neighbors to work for a quantifiable, improved quality of life for all. ▩

Kansas City is a mosaic of neighborhoods covering two states, 11 counties, and 136 communities. Kansas City, Missouri, alone has more than 300 unique and distinct neighborhoods, each with its own flavor and charm, architecture and history.

The area of Strawberry Hill is most closely defined with the South Slavic immigrants, especially the Croatians, who came to the Kansas City area in the late 19th century to seek greater opportunity and prosperity. As was the case for many ethnic communities, life in Strawberry Hill at first resembled life in the old country. Although many changes have occurred, it remains a strong ethnic community and a center for Croatian Americans throughout the Kansas City area.

After World War II, young families moved into the suburbs, where they found affordable housing. The boom continues today in such places as Shawnee, Kansas. Suburban populations have more than tripled in the last three decades.

"Our employees' commitment to their community meshes perfectly with State Street's own commitment to the communities where we do business. Our volunteer-driven Community Service Program works with more than two dozen organizations. That kind of Kansas City spirit is a large part of what makes this a good place to live and helps to drive the growth and rejuvenation of Downtown, the River Market, and the Crossroads district here in the heart of the city."

W. Andrew Fry
Senior Vice President and Managing Director State Street—Kansas City

© Eric R. Berndt, MIDWESTOCK

© Jeff Morgan, MIDWESTOCK

Flowering trees add beauty and grace to Springtime in many Kansas City neighborhoods.

© Kevin Sink, MIDWESTOCK

(Above) The Strawberry Hill Museum and Cultural Center, an original Queen Anne-style home built in 1887, preserves the diverse ethnic cultures that immigrants from Eastern Europe brought to the city in the early 1900s. The museum hosts various exhibits of original art, music, and dance from many cultures.

(Right) Established as a place for relaxation and reflection, Loose Park has playgrounds for children, but also features a miniature lake, footbridge, walking paths, and elegant rose garden. The park is located just south of the Country Club Plaza.

© Bruce Mathews, MIDWESTOCK

© Jeff Morgan, MIDWESTOCK

Kansas City residents and their four-legged companions enjoy strolling through scenic neighborhoods.

Kansas City residents
can find many ways to
invest their leisure time.

*(Following page)
Some Kansas City area
neighborhoods have
seen the changing of
many seasons. Their
residents enjoy stately
established trees that
provide shade in sum-
mer and color in fall.*

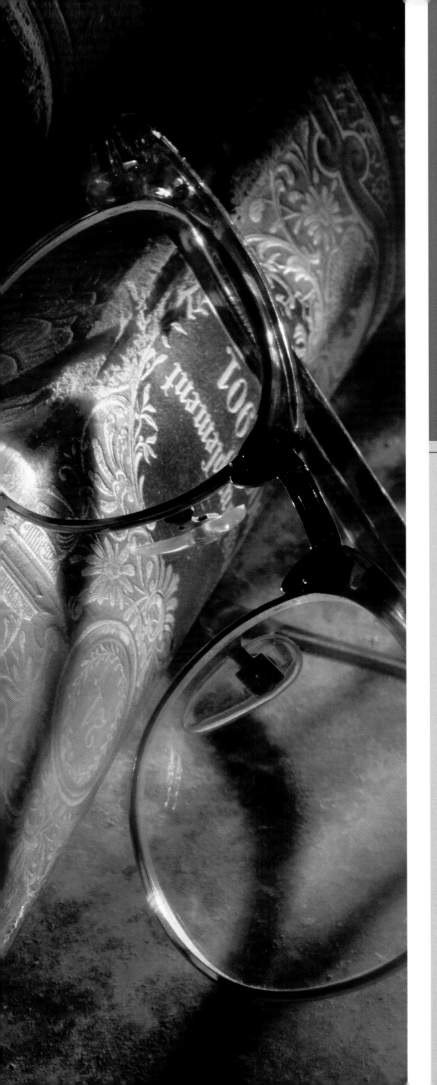

3

Chapter Three

AN EDUCATIONAL FOUNDATION

From early childhood education through graduate schools, Kansas City offers many choices for young and old to learn and study. © Michael Rush, MIDWESTOCK

K ansas Citians have a variety of educational opportunities for any stage of life and any ambition. Institutions of higher learning in the region consistently rank high in assessments of "best buys in education" nationwide. And schools and programs for learners from toddlers to seniors are recognized nationally for excellence.

Before a child even steps into a classroom, area programs are available to help prepare children and parents for unlimited opportunities through education. The Greater Kansas City area, home to nearly 130,000 children under the age of five, in the 1990s made a community-wide commitment to become the "child capital of opportunity."

Many area organizations are dedicated to improving education so critical to the quality of life for children. Annually, the Partnership for Children grades the region in child health, safety, education, and childcare, pointing to areas that need improvement and recognizing achievement. The Greater Kansas City Community Foundation has teamed with partners in business, education, health, and philanthropy in a focused initiative to build an early childhood care and educational system anticipated to be unsurpassed in the nation.

Several of the 65 public school districts in the 11-county region have been nationally acclaimed for their

Founded in 1849, William Jewell College in Liberty, Missouri, has been classified as one of the nation's top 162 liberal arts colleges by the Carnegie Foundation for the Advancement of Teaching. It built a reputation for excellence by bringing together bright, highly motivated students from across the world and giving them the opportunity to excel.

quality, curricula, and special programs. These districts, which serve nearly 300,000 children in grades K-12, fare extremely well on *Expansion Management's* annual education quotient survey of 1,500 districts nationwide for districts that deserve to attract relocating families.

Throughout the metro area, innovative programs and close attention to meeting and exceeding state education standards—as well as the expectations of parents—give children from pre-school through high school academic preparation and life skills.

The Kansas City School District offers varied curriculum choices through its magnet school program, the most ambitious in the nation. The program combines basic skills with specially themed curricula designed to attract additional students to the district and provide more opportunities. The Kansas City, Missouri, School District has magnet schools offering specialized learning opportunities from language-based themes to advanced engineering and technology. The Montessori magnets, for preschool through fifth grades, were the first two public Montessori schools in the country.

Approval of charter school legislation in 1998 provided an alternative approach within public school education. Kansas City ranked first in the nation for the number of approved charter schools that opened during the first year following the passage of the legislation. Kansas City has 19 approved charter schools, with 6,800 students enrolled in fall 2002.

Some of the most successful schools in the nation— ranked by student test scores—and some of the fastest growing districts are located in the region's suburban school districts. One of five Missouri schools nationally designated as Blue Ribbon Schools is in Parkville, Missouri. And *Expansion Management Magazine* designated the Park Hill School District a "Gold Medal District." All of Kansas' Blue Ribbon schools are in Johnson County, which has three of Kansas's largest districts. Cities such as Olathe, Kansas, for the past several years have been building new schools to accommodate population growth.

More than 100 private and parochial schools offer parents and students alternatives to public education. Steady growth in the independent school sector accommodates many philosophies of education and reflects the importance families place on choice. A high level of cooperation exists among these schools, which have set up an association to share materials, facilities, and expertise.

Private schools represent a broad range of interests and ethnic diversity among students, who come from neighborhoods all over the metropolitan area and represent every economic level. Private school alternatives include private college preparatory institutions such as the Barstow School, founded in 1884, and the Pembroke Hill School, formed as a co-educational school in 1983 after seventy-five years as separate girls' and boys' academies.

© Bruce Mathews, MIDWESTOCK

Park University was founded in 1875 as an independent, liberal arts, four-year coeducational, residential Christian institution. Mackay Hall houses the School of Arts and Sciences. The home campus is situated in the small town of Parkville on the bluffs of the Missouri River, fifteen minutes northwest of downtown Kansas City.

Many area private schools have a religious orientation. More than sixty parochial schools serve students from families with particular faith orientations, as well as other students. The Hyman Brand Hebrew Academy, Kansas City's only Jewish community day school and one of a very few such schools west of the Mississippi, provides Judaic and general studies. The Catholic Church of Kansas City opened its first school in 1859, making its system the region's oldest continuously operating educational entity. St. Teresa's Academy, founded in 1866 and owned and operated by the Sisters of St. Joseph of Carondelet, is the oldest parochial school in the city. Bethany Lutheran Church school, begun in school year 2000-2001, is the newest. Together they represent the region's lasting commitment to educational choice and interest in values-based educational programs.

More than 60 percent of respondents to a quality of life survey in Kansas City said that the availability of outstanding higher education is very important in their lives. Within a 50-mile radius of downtown Kansas City, postsecondary students can take advantage of community colleges, private four-year colleges, state universities, two law schools, a conservatory of music, an art institute, four theological colleges, a dental school, and three medical schools. These institutions offer a comprehensive array of programs: two-year associate's and four-year bachelor's degrees, technical and business degrees, master's, law, doctoral, medical, and dental degrees in various professional fields. Outstanding higher education opportunity is reflected in the fact that the number of area

Penn Valley Community College's diverse student body enjoys more than 70 transfer and specialty career degree options as well as short-term certificate programs.

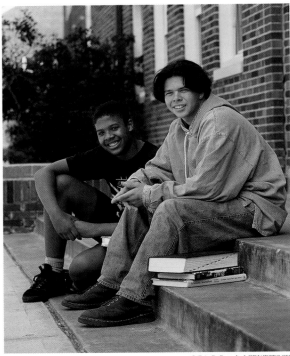

© Eric R. Berndt, MIDWESTOCK

residents who have earned a four-year degree or higher is roughly 21 percent higher than the national average.

Area community colleges play an important role in the learning community. Since 1915, hundreds of thousands of people have attended Kansas City's publicly funded colleges such as the Metropolitan Community Colleges, Johnson County Community Colleges, and Kansas City, Kansas, Community College. They offer two-year degree programs that support the technical needs of businesses and industries as well as provide the fundamentals for students going on to further college work. Community colleges also provide quality instruction, low cost, convenience, and wide range of educational programs.

Kansas City also has five private four-year liberal arts colleges: Avila College, Mid-America Nazarene College, and Rockhurst University in Kansas City, Missouri; Park University in Parkville, Missouri; and William Jewell College in Liberty, Missouri. Baker University, with a main campus in Baldwin, Kansas, provides degree programs in the metro area, as do St. Mary's College, with a main campus in Leavenworth, Kansas, and Ottawa University, headquartered in Ottawa, Kansas. DeVry Institute of Technology offers degrees related to technology, accounting, and business systems.

Research, learning, and industry development are historically and increasingly important assets to the quality and economic growth of the city. Kansas City's public colleges and universities provide education and training to students at several levels, from certificate to associate degree to graduate and professional levels.

One of the Metropolitan Community Colleges

Penn Valley Community College

© John Blasdel, MIDWESTOCK

Chartered in 1929 and established in 1933, the University of Missouri-Kansas City's College of Arts and Sciences leads many students toward professional schools of biological sciences, business and public administration, dentistry, education, law, medicine, nursing and pharmacy; music; and programs in engineering and computer science telecommunications.

© Bob Greenspan, MIDWESTOCK

Rooted in a 450-year-old Jesuit educational tradition, Rockhurst University serves about 3,000 students. The school's graduate business programs rank among the best in the nation.

© Jeff Morgan, MIDWESTOCK

© Jeff Morgan, MIDWESTOCK

(Left) Epperson House was donated by J.J. Lynn to the University of Missouri-Kansas City in 1943 for the purpose of housing Naval cadets during the years of World War II. College legend holds this mansion is haunted by the adopted daughter of Mr. and Mrs. U.S. Epperson.

(Below) Baker University was founded in 1858 by the Methodist Church. Money Magazine *rated it as one of its "Top 100 Colleges & Universities in the U.S."* Baron's Magazine *selected Baker as a "Best Buy for College Education," and* U.S. News and World Report *extended a highest ranking to it, commending it as one of "America's Best Colleges."*

© Bruce Mathews, MIDWESTOCK

More than 45,000 graduates of the University of Kansas live and work in the Kansas City area. KU, located in Lawrence, a 45-minute drive from downtown Kansas City, Missouri, significantly influences the region's life in commerce, medicine, the arts, science, government, education, and sports. In the Kansas City area, KU also offers master's degree programs at the KU Edwards Campus in Overland Park, and operates the University of Kansas Medical School in Kansas City, Kansas, a teaching, research, and patient care institution.

The University of Missouri-Kansas City is one of four campuses in the University of Missouri system and is a leading source of professional and advanced graduate study. Chartered in 1929 and established in 1933, UMKC's College of Arts and Sciences leads many students toward

the campus' professional schools of Biological Sciences, Business and Public Administration, Dentistry, Education, Law, Medicine, Nursing, and Pharmacy; the Conservatory of Music; and programs in engineering and computer science telecommunications.

Kansas City is a community committed to education—a community constantly striving to increase educational opportunities for all of its citizenry. Perhaps no other topic fuels area conversation as much as education. Committed attention by parents and other adults creates the shared responsibility required to achieve the goals of the region's twenty-first century schools.

© Bruce Mathews, MIDWESTOCK

© Bruce Mathews, MIDWESTOCK

Johnson County Community College is Kansas' largest community college and is the third largest institution of higher learning in Kansas with a spring 2001 enrollment of 16,777.

With some of the finest schools in the nation located within the metropolitan region, children can be assured many opportunities to develop intellectually, socially, and artistically.

"Learning is a constant pursuit for successful people and enterprises. At American Century, we are committed to enhancing the quality of life in our community by supporting and providing educational opportunities. We believe it is important to challenge people to explore new ways of thinking, and then to share their knowledge and experience to help others succeed."

William M. Lyons
President and CEO
American Century Companies

*The North Kansas City
School District provides
learning activities to
foster a respect for
diversity and opportu-
nities for students to
expand their under-
standing and accept-
ance of self and others.*

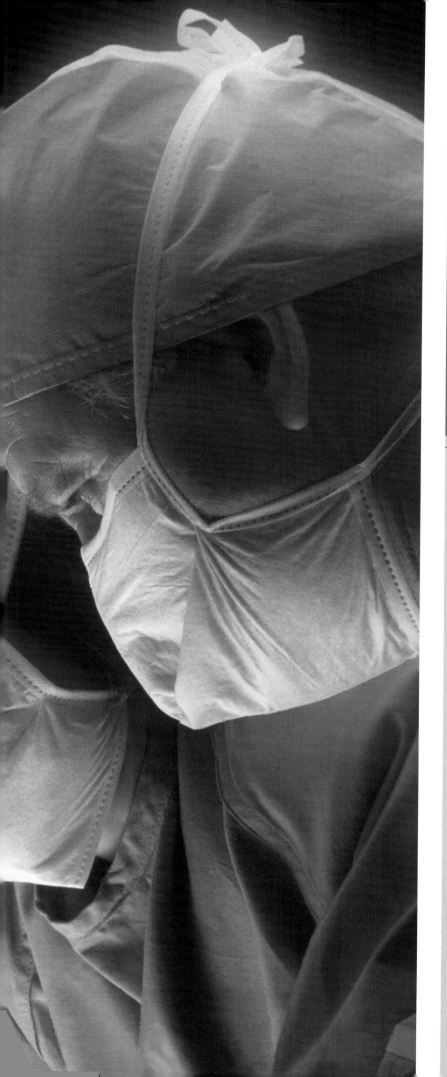

4

Chapter Four

A HEALTHY TOMORROW

Kansas City has an extensive medical and health care
network of physicians, nurses, and technicians who
provide the finest care possible in many specialties.

© Don Wolf, MIDWESTOCK

Greater Kansas City has a national reputation for barbeque, greeting cards, jazz, and professional sports. Soon the city will be able to add another claim to fame: its status as a world-class medical research center where scientists probe the causes and formulate cures for ravaging diseases and disabilities.

Kansas City took a giant step into the life sciences arena with the 2000 opening of the $200 million Stowers Institute for Medical Research. Located just east of the Country Club Plaza, the Stowers Institute for Medical Research aspires to be one of the most innovative biomedical research facilities in the world. The Institute conducts basic research into complex genetic systems to unlock the mysteries of disease and find the keys to their causes, treatment and prevention. Jim and Virginia Stowers, two cancer survivors who decided to dedicate their fortune to supporting the basic research that will provide long-term solutions to gene-based diseases, founded it. The Institute is a gift to the city where their mutual funds firm, American Century Companies, was born and nurtured.

Eventually, the Stowers Institute will house forty to fifty independent research programs in its Kansas City facility, each with an average of ten to twelve scientists, research associates, and technicians—making a total of about six hundred people including other support staff and the administrative team. The Institute opened with four independent research programs in November 2000 and continues to add new ones. By the end of 2002, the Institute will have up to twenty independent research programs and 250 scientists, researcher associates, technicians, and support staff.

The Stowers Institute is not an isolated venture. The Institute has linked with the University of Kansas Medical Center, the University of Missouri-Kansas City, and Midwest Research Institute to attract people, funding, and other resources for life sciences. This is an example of ways in which Kansas City's strength in healthcare is increasing steadily through alliances and partnerships.

With a $27 million gift from the Hall Family Foundation, the University of Kansas Medical Center is building a new research facility for brain research, genetic medicine, and protein research. The University of Kansas and the University of Missouri-Kansas City have also formed a partnership for research in life and health sciences and for life sciences programs for students from kindergarten through high school and even into community college.

The life sciences initiative builds on the region's historic foundation in excellent health care provided by universities, medical and nursing schools, area hospitals, and health care centers. Each year thousands of people from across the country come to Kansas City seeking accurate diagnoses, effective treatment, and compassionate care for a wide variety of health challenges. The area's eighty thousand doctors, nurses, technicians, and support staff in health care centers provide up-to-date facilities and expertise—the best available medical care. These hospitals treat more than 205,000 in-care patients each year, deliver about twenty-six thousand babies, and offer the latest in treatment, technology, and wellness programs.

As a regional center, Kansas City draws patients from across the Midwest. More than twenty-seven thousand people admitted annually to area hospitals come from outside the metropolitan area. For these as well as local residents, the metro area offers scores of acute care hospitals, including those with Level II Trauma Centers, as well as independent rehabilitation facilities, psychiatric hospitals, more than a dozen public health clinics, a veterans' hospital, and a world-class children's hospital. In addition, the Kansas City area has award-winning emergency medical technicians who offer life saving treatment for cardiac patients on their way to emergency rooms, and Life Flight Eagle helicopters that transport critical patients within a 50-mile radius to appropriate medical facilities. The area's primary provider to the

Cutting-edge technology, such as imaging computers, enables Kansas City's health care professionals to diagnose and treat diseases and injuries accurately and effectively.

© Michael Rush, MIDWESTOCK

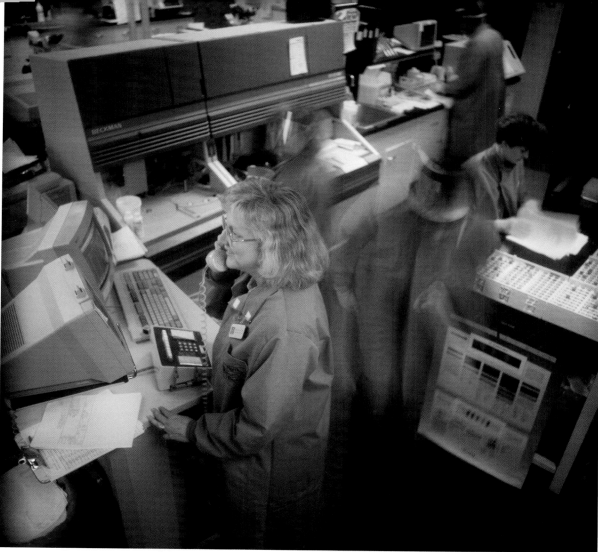

medically indigent, Swope Parkway Health Center, operates a mobile health clinic to deliver health care services even to people who are homeless.

Kansas City provides many other health-related services and businesses: home health services, hospice care, retirement centers, centers for mental health and developmental disabilities, and fitness facilities. There are three medical schools, a dental school, ten nursing schools, and several allied health training programs in the area. Global pharmaceutical companies, laboratories, equipment manufacturers, and health information companies have offices and other facilities here. The area boasts leaders in animal health care research and new product development as well.

As a community, Kansas Citians understand that their best assets are their children. This value is reflected in the many pediatric clinics and health programs throughout the region. Kansas City is home to Children's Mercy Hospital, the nation's largest provider of pediatric outpatient care, treating more than two hundred thousand children as outpatients each year. The area also has several programs aimed at wellness in babies and improving childhood development, such as the Healthy Steps for Young Children Program at the University of Kansas Medical Center. Healthy Steps seeks to connect parents with pediatricians and trained early childhood specialists who teach parents appropriate brain stimulation techniques for their infants and toddlers.

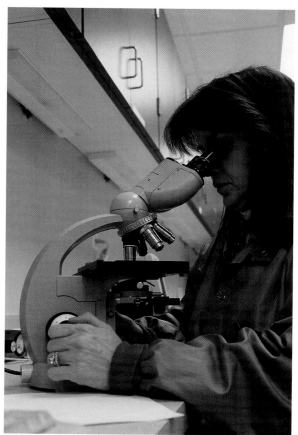

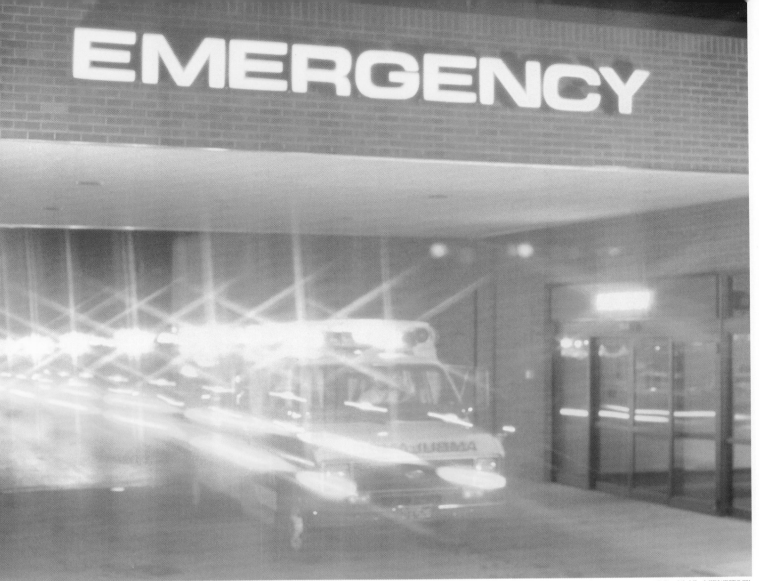

EMERGENCY

Award-winning emergency medical services providers offer life saving treatment on their way to one of Kansas City's many acute care facilities, including Level II Trauma Centers, where medical teams deliver advanced care to critically ill and injured patients.

As health care costs have escalated in recent years, provider systems have replaced most independent medical facilities in an effort to improve efficiencies and enhance effectiveness. Kansas City has three large health care systems: Health Midwest, Saint Luke's Health System, and St. Louis-based Carondelet Health System.

Health Midwest encompasses fifteen acute care hospitals and regional health care centers within a 150-mile radius of Kansas City, Missouri. The flagship hospital is Research Medical Center. Research has pioneered many treatments and procedures, including the Midwest Gamma Knife Center, which transformed high-risk brain surgery into an outpatient procedure. Also in this system are Menorah Medical Center, the Overland Park Regional Medical Center, and the Rehabilitation Institute of Kansas City, which provides wide-ranging programs for area children and adults with disabilities.

The Saint Luke's-Shawnee Mission Health Care System represents the merger in 1996 of the Shawnee Mission Medical Center, in Overland Park and Saint Luke's Hospital, which traces its beginnings to 1882 as the community's first hospital. The two institutions were at the time the area's largest in admissions and outpatient procedures. Today the system consists of eight area hospitals and more than fourteen physician and health provider offices throughout the Kansas City area. The system

"At KPMG, we've had the privilege of serving some of the best health-care companies in Kansas City and have seen the truly amazing accomplishments of this industry in our community. The economic impact to our market, which is significant, is not the full story.

"When considering this industry, you have to consider the advances by local research facilities that protect our families from debilitating illnesses; you have to consider the miracles that are produced every hour of every day in every hospital, without fail; and to consider the miracles and the millions of lives saved— you have to revere the industry's countless heroes."

David M. Fowler,
Managing Partner
KPMG

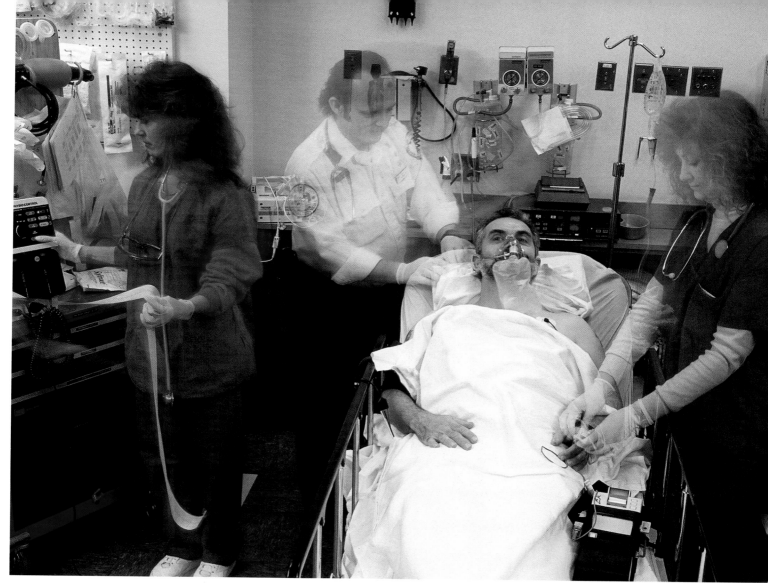

includes Saint Luke's Hospital of Kansas City, one of the nation's leading private teaching hospitals; Mid America Heart Institute, the region's premier cardiac center; Crittenton, Kansas City's leading provider of psychiatric care for children and their families; and the popular Ask-A-Nurse service, a 24-hour medical information line that has fielded more than one million calls about health care.

The lead hospital for the Carondelet Health Systems in Kansas City is St. Joseph Health Center. Founded in 1874, St. Joseph is the oldest private hospital in Kansas City. Carondelet also operates St. Mary's Hospital in Blue Springs and three skilled and intermediate care nursing facilities in the Greater Kansas City area.

Allied with Children's Mercy in delivering comprehensive health care services care to people in need is Truman Medical Center. Truman Medical Center Hospital Hill is probably best known for its excellence in emergency and trauma services. It operates the busiest adult emergency department in the Kansas City area, receiving more than fifty thousand patients a year, and is a Level I (highest designation) trauma center. TMC Hospital Hill, Truman Medical Center Lakewood and Truman Medical Center Behavioral Health Network make up the Truman Medical Centers network. It provides a full-range of quality health care services, including dental and mental health, to Kansas City residents who are indigent and uninsured.

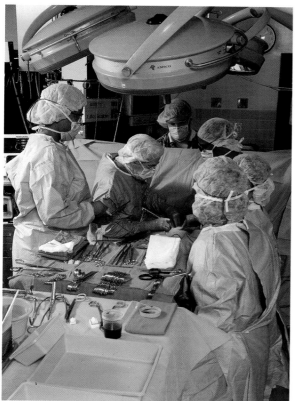

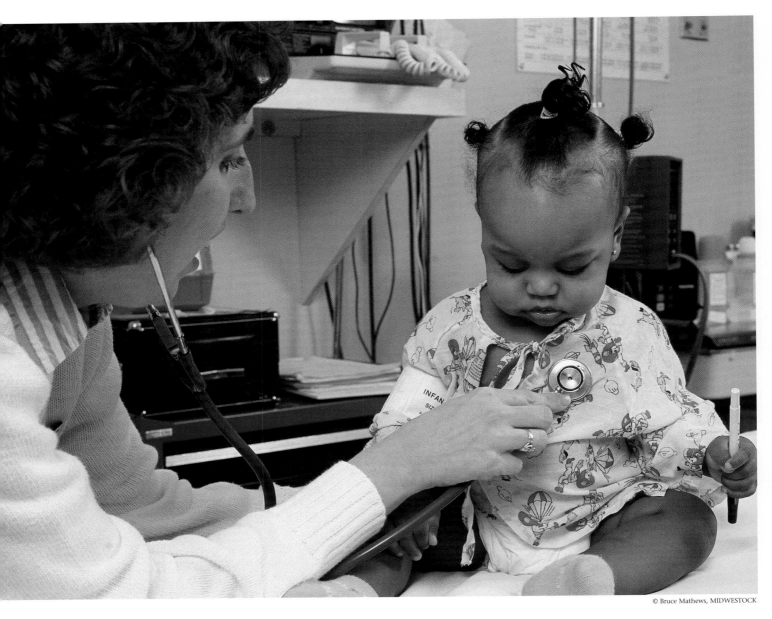

Kansas Citians place a top priority on the wellness and care of their children. Children's Mercy Hospital in Kansas City, Missouri, treats more than 200,000 children as outpatients each year. The hospital recently raised $53 million toward its pediatric research efforts.

Many community hospitals also offer comprehensive health services, including Independence Regional, North Kansas City Hospital, and Kindred Hospital.

Good health ranks as one of the most important quality of life issues for residents of Greater Kansas City regardless of income or neighborhood. Wellness and prevention are a focus for health care institutions and individuals and the area boasts a high percentage of health professionals. In fact, Kansans live in one of the statistically healthiest states in the nation.

Still, the goal of the providers is to explore ways to make care, health, and health care better. One of the challenges facing Kansas City area leadership is making sure everyone has access to affordable, quality health care.

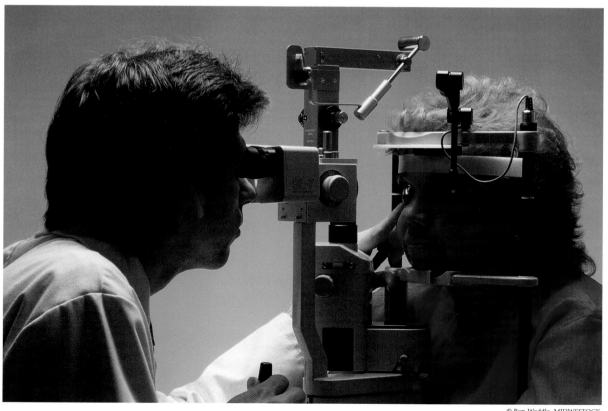

Kansas City area residents have access to a multitude of health care specialists for preventative and treatment medicine ranging from optometry to podiatry.

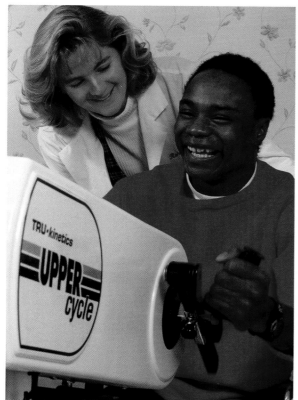

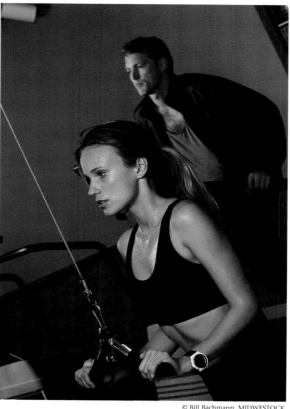

(Opposite) For older residents, the region offers numerous retirement centers, assisted living facilities, and nursing homes to meet their need for chronic and skilled care. Programs such as "pets for patients" aim at meeting seniors' social, emotional, and physical needs.

(This page) Kansas Citians are among the nation's healthiest workers, in part due to the quality of care throughout all stages of life. Clinics, rehabilitation centers, fitness centers, routine blood pressure checks, and mental health centers combine to meet the community's health needs.

5

Chapter Five

IN GOOD FAITH

One flickering flame of faith combined with others can light the darkest day. Indeed, the spiritual devotion of Kansas City residents has sustained them through floods, tornados, war, and other trials and has often been the vehicle to bring people together to serve a common cause. © JoAnn Frederick, MIDWESTOCK

From primitive brick missions to the establishment of inspiring world headquarters, people in Kansas City's communities of faith express deeply held beliefs through their generosity, their prayers, their kindness, their music, their theologies, and their celebrations.

Faith traditions began early in Kansas City's history. The Cathedral of the Immaculate Conception at 12th Street and Broadway is the oldest worshiping congregation of Kansas City, tracing its origins to services conducted in a log cabin in 1834. Methodists, Quakers, and Baptists sent missionaries to the region before the Civil War to spread the Gospel, build schools, and establish new congregations.

From the work of these early faithful grew great congregations and an ecumenical spirit that has made Kansas City home to more than a dozen faiths from around the world—Roman Catholic, Protestant, Jewish, Islam, Eastern Orthodox, Hindu, Buddhist, Sufi, Baha'I, Native American, Sikh, Jain, Unitarian Universalists, and Scientology. More than twelve hundred different types of congregations meet in churches, cathedrals, synagogues, temples, storefronts, gymnasiums, private homes, tents, stadiums, and arenas for worship activities ranging from intimate prayer circles of two or three to services for thousands.

Several denominational world headquarters are located here. The Community of Christ—formerly known as the Reorganized Church of Latter Day Saints—established its headquarters in Independence in 1920 and today has 27,161 members and 81 congregations in the Greater Kansas City area. The impressive temple, with its 300-foot spire and 102-rank pipe organ, stands near a 6,000-seat auditorium and a 110-rank organ, one of the largest in the world.

Another landmark world headquarters near Lee's Summit, Missouri, is the Unity School of Christianity, founded by Charles and Myrtle Fillmore in 1899. A 165-foot Italian Renaissance tower in the middle of the garden campus serves as a carillon, a water tower, and an office building. Visitors from around the world come to the campus for weddings in the beautiful gardens or for spiritual retreats.

The Nazarene Church world headquarters in midtown Kansas City, Missouri, also houses a publishing house established in 1912 that has grown into one of the largest religious publishers in the world. The campus is also home to Nazarene College, which offers degrees in theology and education.

The religious bodies help hold Kansas City together through many shared values, commitments to ethical behavior, and the acknowledgement of being connected to someone or something larger than themselves. According to a recent Mid-America Regional Council survey, 70 percent of those surveyed consider strong morals and ethics to be extremely important to their lives in the metroplex.

Open doors and warm welcomes greet Kansas City worshipers as they gather each week for services.

Kansas City families seek communion with God and each other through prayer, praise, and song in synagogues and churches.

Within the diversity of faiths is a willingness to come together to build community through interfaith groups, observances, conferences, and festivals. The National Day of Prayer, the Ministerial Association's annual interfaith Thanksgiving services, and the United Prayer Movement welcome all who come to participate. Interfaith cooperation and ecumenical activities have long been important to Kansas City's religious life. The first recorded exchange of pulpits was in 1890 when Episcopal Bishop B.B. Usher of Christ Church spoke at B'nai Jehudah and Rabbi Henry Berkowitz returned the visit. On St. Patrick's Day in 1895, Rabbi Samuel Schulman was the principal speaker at a gathering in Kansas City of three thousand Irish-American Catholics. His theme of "reverence for the sacredness of conscience" was a philosophy that has permeated the religious life of Kansas City for more than a hundred years.

For many within the different religious bodies, an important dimension to their faith is the call to give and care for others. These people provide homeless shelters, soup kitchens, food pantries, clothing closets, counseling, money to pay heating bills, and other helping hand activities. Many of the area's fine hospitals, such as Saint Luke's Hospital, Shawnee Mission Medical Center, Menorah Medical Center, St. Joseph Health Center, Baptist Medical Center, and St. Mary's Hospital of Blue Springs were established and supported by communities of faith. Religious groups also created orphanages. The Gillis Home for children, for example, was started by the Women's Christian Temperance Union in 1883.

One of the most extensive and innovative religious groups was Jewish immigrants, primarily from the German Reform origin. Early Jewish settlers set in place a

model for the social welfare infrastructure of the greater Kansas City community. In 1901, the United Jewish Charities was formed to consolidate assistance efforts, not just for Jewish people, but for anyone in need.

Another faith community that built a number of lasting charitable institutions was the Roman Catholic Church. Catholic Family and Children's Services began when Kansas City's first priest, Father Bernard Donnelly, organized assistance programs for Catholics arriving to the area. Today, they carry on the same caring tradition.

The Metropolitan Lutheran Ministries also affirms the rights of people to food, clothing, and shelter, while promoting self-sufficiency and hope through direct services and advocacy. Anchored by fifty congregations of the Evangelical Lutheran Church of America and the Lutheran Church-Missouri Synod, a total of 117 congregations from twelve denominations and four synagogues, support their work.

The region's religious heritage abounds with traditional acts of kindness that continue to improve the quality of life for those Kansas City residents who have the greatest need and the least ability to meet that need. Strength of faith is also reflected in the monumental architecture and design of many churches, cathedrals, synagogues, and temples where Kansas Citians gather together with those of similar beliefs to worship, pray, sing, serve, sacrifice, and celebrate. 🔯

(Right) Prayer is one of the many ways Kansas City residents share their faith.

(Opposite) The Community of Christ auditorium in Independence, Missouri, seats 6,000 people and has one of the nation's largest pipe organs. The world headquarters of the denomination were established here in 1920.

© Mark E. Gibson, MIDWESTOCK

"Kansas City is an excellent place to live, work, and play. A Midwestern sense of style combines with metropolitan avenues and a wealth of opportunity to enhance, enrich, and expand minds both professionally and personally. A history of diversity creates a kaleidoscope of cultural, religious, and economic visions that lend a richness rarely found in most communities. Residents and visitors choose from such attractions as the American Jazz Museum, 18th & Vine Historic District, Worlds of Fun and Oceans of Fun Theme parks—not to mention an abundance of galleries, historic sites, museums, professional sports, concerts, theater, festivals, churches, synagogues, and more. Truly, we are a community blessed."

C.L. "Book" Lawrence
Corporate Communications
U.S. Public Relations
Community Affairs Manager
Williams Companies

From historic chapels with roots in the 1800s to 21st century "mega-churches" under construction in the suburbs, Kansas City residents find almost unlimited opportunities and places to worship together. © Susan Pfannmuller, MIDWESTOCK

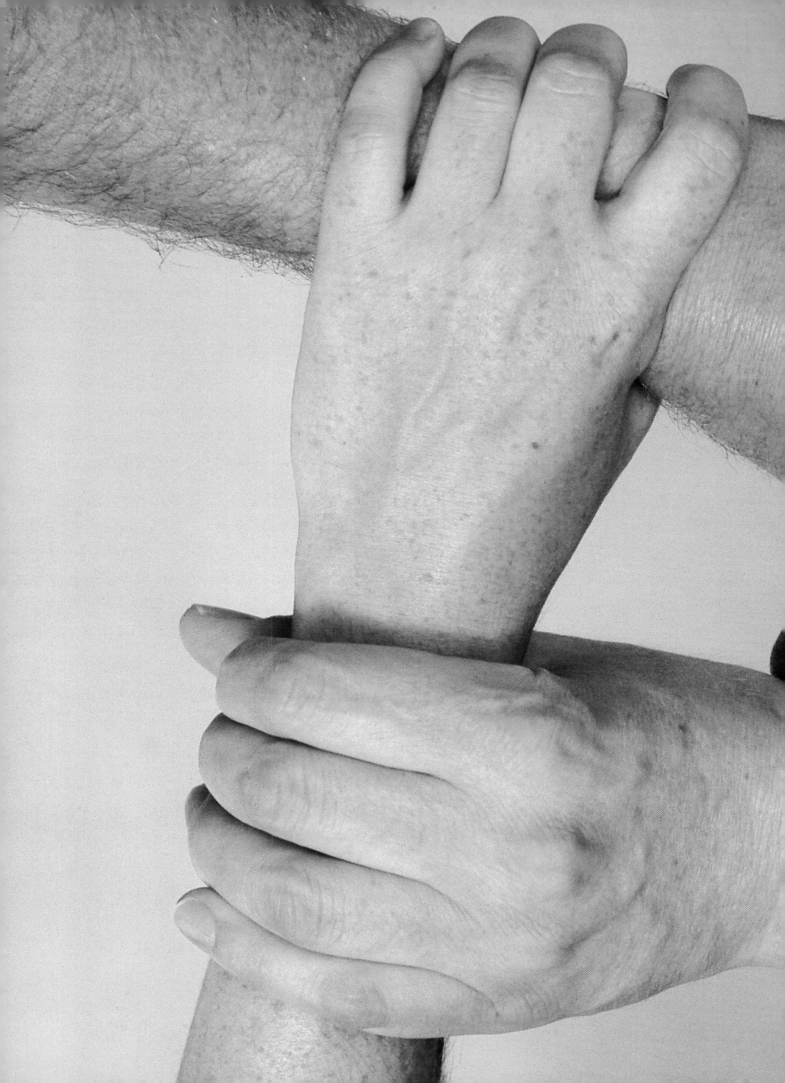

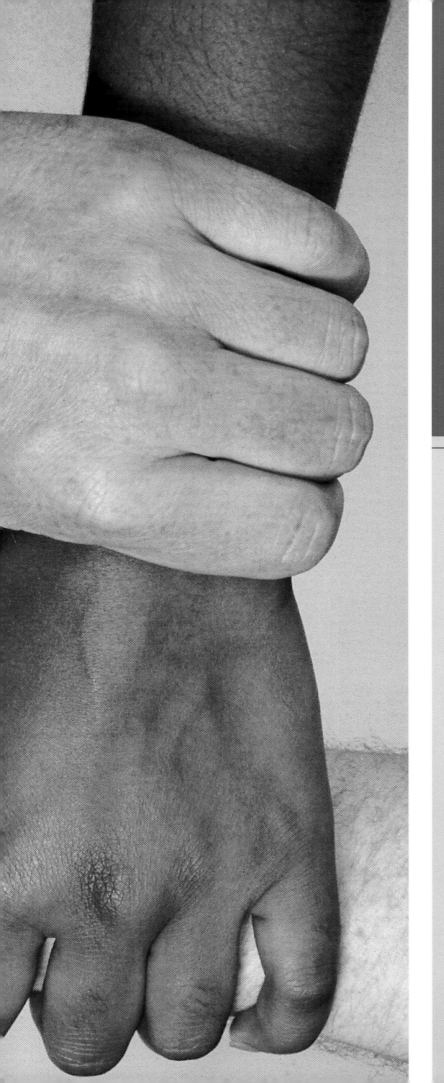

6

Chapter Six

HELPING HANDS

Kansas City residents have a well-earned reputation for helping each other. These hands represent teamwork, strength, and cooperation when people join forces to overcome adversity.

© Novastock/MIDWESTOCK

K ansas Citians seem to be born with a generous spirit. They are innately generous in giving, not just money, but of themselves, their time, and their talents to help neighbors, friends, even strangers. Increasingly donors large and small are investigating ways to give wisely and to make lasting change. They are ready to address big issues—such as the quality of life for all area children—and to expect measurable difference when they invest in a cause.

But area residents are also willing to do the hands-on work of charity, however small. They pitch in, form brigades, bake cookies, brainstorm for hours, stuff envelopes, make phone calls, pound nails, and run marathons. They put on black ties and evening gowns for galas and charity balls. They give blood and pull rumpled dollars from their pockets to stuff into firefighters' boots. They build fountains and bring headliner acts to town. They drive vans, deliver meals, telephone shut-ins, visit the sick, and serve food at soup kitchens.

Philanthropist Ewing M. Kauffman expressed it this way: "All the money in the world cannot solve problems unless we work together. And, if we work together, there is no problem in the world that can stop us as we seek to develop people to the highest and best potential."

Kauffman, who built his pharmaceutical company from a few thousand dollars in annual sales to well over $3 billion, knew that generosity was more than writing a check. It was getting personally involved in

© Eric R. Berndt, MIDWESTOCK

Hundreds of volunteers show up each fall for "Christmas in October" to repair and improve homes of those in need.

(Right) Many Kansas Citians seek opportunities to give back to the community that has been so good to them.

(Opposite) Kansas City residents practice good stewardship of their environment through many activities, such as recycling papers on Earth Day or cleaning litter from city streets.

© Jim Hays, MIDWESTOCK

the community, with its people, and with its needs. Kauffman left an enduring legacy through the foundation that bears his name. With assets exceeding $1.7 billion, Ewing Marion Kauffman Foundation today is one of the largest foundations in the nation. The foundation uses its gifts towards developing self-sufficient people in healthy communities, primarily focusing on youth development and entrepreneurial leadership.

Community is distinguished by many philanthropic entities that provide leadership in community policy and practice and millions of dollars in charitable funding annually. The Hall Family Foundation, one of the region's largest and most influential charitable entities, concentrates on such areas of local emphasis as support of major visual and performing arts institutions, community development in the urban core, civic and community issues of high priority, and education.

Other area major foundations include the H & R Block Foundation, the Francis Families Foundation, Murial McBrien Kauffman Foundation, the William T. and Charlotte Kemper Foundation, the Hallmark Corporate Foundation, the Catholic Community Foundation, and many more.

Altogether, the region has nearly six hundred foundations and philanthropies that support a wide variety of important causes and programs in the fields of medical

Runners compete each year in the Trolley Run, the largest four-mile run in the nation. Money raised in the race is donated to Children's Mercy Hospital.

research and healthcare, arts and culture, education and scholarships, early childhood development and at-risk youth, museums, gardens and fountains, inner city neighborhoods, and regional historic sites.

Kansas Citians rank among the most generous people in the United States, each year giving above the national average to support their charitable interests. In the Greater Kansas City area, 75 percent of all households and 79 percent of all businesses give annually to non-profit organizations.

Since 1978, the Greater Kansas City Community Foundation has worked to improve the quality of life in the region. It accomplishes this through an active partnership with donors and others who believe that positive change can occur through effective charitable giving. Today, the Community Foundation manages more than 1,500 charitable funds started by individuals, families, businesses, and nonprofit organizations. Together, these funds represent ordinary people who have made extraordinary commitments to our community. In the year 2000, the GKCCF and the Kauffman Foundation together gave $197 million in grants to non-profit organizations.

Most area foundations are the result of business success or family wealth that makes possible significant philanthropy. But the area is rich with examples of significant acts of giving that began with one or two people who simply wanted to help. Virjean Burton, for example, put together a few thousand dollars in the late 1980s to help families and children living in the Northland. That gift has grown into more than $16 million in the Northland Community Fund.

Other times the need to give grows out of having received. Kim and Nate Harbur of Overland Park started the Gift of Life Foundation to promote awareness of organ and tissue donations after their young son's life was saved through a liver transplant.

Other people simply see an opportunity to assist and act on it. That's what happened in 1984 when attorney Richard W. Miller and John P. McMeel, president of Andrews and McMeel Universal, saw a way to help Kansas City residents stay in their own homes. They founded "Christmas in October," a concentrated community wide effort that draws scores of volunteers each fall to fix up hundreds of houses for low-income homeowners.

Historically, the passion to help others came with the territory. The people who chose to live near the confluence of the Missouri and Kansas rivers likewise came together as one body again and again to overcome disasters, to encourage others toward achievement, to help those who were down on their luck, or to enhance the quality of life. Whether it was raising a barn, nursing residents through cholera epidemics, or establishing a new college, the early settlers knew they must cooperate to survive and to build a viable society for their children and grandchildren. They needed courage, resolve, and magnanimous spirits to overcome floods, to outlast waves of communicable diseases that swept through town, and to bring the finer things of life to a town where barrooms and brothels often passed for culture.

Later, when the town was well on its way to becoming a major population center in the Heart of America, other Kansas Citians stepped up to meet the needs of those less fortunate as well as improve the community's quality of

The Bloch Cancer Survivors Park on the Country Club Plaza serves as rallying spot for area residents who have battled and survived cancer.

life. Concerned women established orphanages. One man built the finest opera house between the Mississippi and San Francisco. Another donated land for what is still the nation's second largest urban park. And another helped establish the first board of public welfare in the United States.

Not only the wealthy did their part. People from all economic levels and backgrounds participated in making Kansas City a better place to live. Two sisters who were doctors established the area's first hospital for crippled children. To support them, more than three hundred women's clubs throughout the Midwest raised money by selling home-canned fruit and handmade quilts. Today, their Children's Mercy Hospital is one of the world's finest pediatric hospitals and the recipient of hundreds of millions of donated dollars over the years, including a recent $40 million gift from the Hall Family Foundations.

This is a community that has long understood the need to share and to share in a timely fashion, when need presents itself. A defining event took place at the end of World War I, when people throughout town were so moved to pay tribute to the nation's wounded and dead that they donated a remarkable $2.5 million in just ten days in 1919 to build what is still the nation's only World War I combined memorial and museum.

Not much has changed at the heart of Greater Kansas City. Although area residents live in a pell-mell world of Web sites, cell phones, and drive-throughs, they remain civic-minded, compassionate folks. In a recent survey, the vast majority of Kansas Citians indicated they still want the good life not just for themselves, but for everyone in town. The people in the Heart of America instinctively

continue to reach out in times of crisis or celebrations, even if they've never shaken hands or know one another's names. They do what is required—and then some. Whatever the problem they face, they face it together. ◈

"Kansas City is well-positioned to become a world-class center for biomedical research. A spirit of partnering exits within the life sciences community with institutions cooperating to maximize mutual strengths and resources, significantly contributing to the advancement of this effort. The Life Sciences Initiative will have a profound economic and social impact on a community that is already alive with remarkable spirit. Kansas City is proud of its track record in scientific firsts and technological breakthroughs, and we look forward to many more in the decade ahead."

Karen L. Pletz, J.D.
President and Chief Executive Officer
The University of Health Sciences

The Ewing Marion Kauffman Foundation at 48th Street and Rockhill Road is just one of hundreds of foundations and philanthropies in Kansas City. Established by Ewing Kauffman, founder of Marion Laboratories and former owner of the Kansas City Royals baseball club, the foundation focuses its philanthropic support on youth development and entrepreneurial leadership.

(Right) Dozens of agencies and organizations, including the Salvation Army, provide food, shelter, and support for people who are homeless and others in need.

(Opposite) The Mayor's Christmas Tree at Crown Center is an annual symbol of a fund-raising campaign to provide holiday gifts, clothing, and food items to the city's underprivileged. Each year, the fund assists more than 30,000 people in the Greater Kansas City area, making it one of the biggest contributors to those in need in the community.

AM ROCKHILL NELSON GALLERY OF ART

7

Chapter Seven

A CULTURAL MASTERPIECE

**The neoclassic Nelson-Atkins Museum of Art is known
internationally for its collections of modern sculptures
and Asian art. The lawns serve as a sculpture park for
Henry Moore creations and giant shuttlecocks by Claes
Oldenburg and Coosie van Bruggen.**

© Kevin Sink, MIDWESTOCK

I f commitment to arts and cultural opportunity is the sign of a mature city, Kansas City has grown up. From a rough and tumble town where making money was a primary objective of most civic boosters, Kansas City has learned to rank arts and culture high on the scale of what matters.

Greater Kansas City has more than 250 visual and performing arts organizations that provide ways for people of all ages and economic levels to experience and participate in the arts. Add to that a host of other opportunities: galleries, history museums and sites, sculpture gardens and botanical gardens, literary groups and specialty publications, ethnic and heritage organizations, community center and school-based arts programming, arts offerings through faith communities, professional and community theater productions, outdoor public art and fountains, a wide variety of

Kansas City's many fountains are works of art in their own right as active sculptures. Pictured, Neptune reining in his horses is one of the dozens of fountains that grace the Country Club Plaza.

architectural styles in its public buildings, and the holdings of private and corporate collectors, shared with visitors. The list goes on and on—creating the wonderfully complex tapestry that is Kansas City's arts and cultural life.

In perhaps no other area of endeavor is Kansas City's diversity so obvious—or so rewarding. It surfaces in outdoor art shows, in ethnic festivals and holiday celebrations, in every kind of shared experience, from symphony performances to the sounds of Kansas City jazz coming from a nearby club. This diversity inspires artists and audiences alike and gives Kansas City a cultural dimension of uncommon richness and depth.

Greater Kansas City is a regional cultural center. Increasingly, activities attract patrons from outside the metro area. In 2000, roughly 41 percent of attendees at cultural events were visitors from outside the metroplex or outside both the states of Kansas and Missouri.

Many visitors come to experience the more than sixty area art galleries, museums, and centers that show the work of artists from around the country. The community is home to one of the country's best art museums, one of the nation's finest regional symphonies and more professional theaters than any city of comparable size in the United States. It boasts a splendid ballet company, a busy gallery scene, world-class performing arts facilities, and one of the few opera companies in the world that sings in English.

In addition to elevating the quality of life for residents and visitors, the arts are good business in Kansas City. Cultural organizations are a powerful economic and social force within Greater Kansas City. The economic impact of almost one and a half million out-of-town visitors is enormous. Annually, more than $85 million is brought to Kansas City's economy as people visit museums, historic sites, and attend performing arts events each year.

But the arts contribution to Kansas City cannot be counted only in dollars, especially when Kansas Citians give so much time to the arts. Thousands of volunteers contribute nearly a quarter of a million hours annually to support cultural activities. They provide critical administrative, artistic, and technical expertise to area institutions. The results enrich the community as a whole.

The twenty-first century economy is based on more than money: economists, social scientists, business leaders, and political leaders increasingly emphasize that creativity is the true currency of the new millennium. When asked to rank factors that would most improve their quality of life, Kansas City area residents ranked access to arts and culture ahead of many other life-enhancing factors, including a more affordable house, the availability of quality higher education—even ahead of more challenging and satisfying work.

From the outdoor sculptures and fountains to the varied museums and concert halls, Kansas Citians express their love and appreciation of the arts.

© Kevin Sink, MIDWESTOCK

*(Previous page)
The Folly Theater in
downtown Kansas City
is the area's oldest
playhouse, dating to
1900. The building
was renovated in 1981
and continues today
as a popular perform-
ing arts venue.*

*Jazz permeates
Kansas City culture.
The Majestic Steak
House, one of down-
town Kansas City's
legendary restaurants,
regularly features live
jazz entertainment.*

Nelson-Atkins Museum of Art, a favorite with visitors and locals alike, ranks among the top eight museums in the country and is especially known for its Oriental collection. Always a busy place, the museum mounts special showings from its own collection and hosts traveling exhibits that draw additional crowds. The Nelson continues to develop fine collections and innovative programming through a world-class curatorial staff and generous local patrons. An extraordinary building program is expanding the facility, a Neo-classic landmark surrounded by one of the nation's premier sculpture parks, with innovative architecture that will feature light-filled structures over underground facilities.

Near the Nelson-Atkins in midtown Kansas City is the Kemper Museum of Contemporary Art, a museum open free to the public every day. Exhibits from the permanent collections and traveling exhibits change regularly, attracting residents as repeat visitors to the intimate, innovative museum that features a café, outdoor sculpture, interior courtyard, and museum shop.

The Kansas City Art Institute, founded in 1885, is the oldest arts institution in Kansas City. The private, four-year college trains artists, designers and is the only college of art and design between Chicago and the West Coast. Alumni such as Walt Disney and Robert

(Left and top opposite) *Kansas City jazz was born in the 18th and Vine District in the early 1920s. The Jazz Museum houses the Blue Room, a club where local artists can jam into the night. Across the street is the historic Gem Theater, which has been completely restored for live performances and film exhibits.*

Although the Kansas City Symphony often plays in non-traditional settings, such as parks, its holiday performances in the Music Hall draws hundreds of loyal fans each year.

Rauschenberg have made lasting impressions on American life. The Institute offers regularly changing exhibits.

Many working artists call Kansas City home. The Kansas City Artists Coalition, formed in 1973 to promote visual arts awareness in Kansas City and the surrounding region, presents an outstanding and varied program of visual arts exhibits, panel discussions, workshops, gallery talks, publications, and community outreach. More than sixty area galleries display the work of regional artists, as well as national and international talents. Galleries and antique shops are clustered in some of the city's restored areas, such as the Crossroads District, Westport, the River Market area, and midtown along State Line Road.

Kansas City's rich historical heritage gives museum-goers and history buffs a fascinating variety of offerings. Among the area's more than 250 museums and historic sites are several that provide personal looks at everything

from our nation's thirty-third president, at the Harry S. Truman Library and Museum and the Truman Home in Independence, Missouri, to notorious outlaws at the Jesse James Farm and Museum in nearby Kearney, Missouri. More than 70 percent of the visitors to the area report they are attracted to museums and historic sites.

Much of the city's history has been preserved. Visitors and locals can learn more about the Santa Fe, California, and Oregon trails at the National Frontier Trails Center in Independence, Missouri. Or imagine what life was like in the mid-1800s for settlers moving west by visiting the Arabia Steamboat Museum, where more than 200 tons of buried treasure was recovered from the sunken 1856 steamboat.

The 18th & Vine Historic District shows off Kansas City's musical heritage and baseball tradition. The American Jazz Museum, the Horace M. Peterson Visitors Center, the Gem Theater, and the Negro Leagues Baseball Museum offer visitors a closer look at the rich history of Kansas City jazz and its performers as well as a behind-the-scenes look at the sights, sounds, and experiences of Negro Leagues Baseball.

One of Kansas City's nationally known contributions to the arts is to music. Kansas City's music lovers pack the city's classical, jazz, pop, rock, and country venues year round. The summer's outdoor concert season may be the region's biggest melting pot, attracting more diverse crowds than even sporting events. Big outdoor concerts are a tradition in Kansas City at city parks and in popular venues such as Sandstone Amphitheatre in Bonner Springs, Kansas, where top recording artists perform under the stars.

And the 8,000-seat Starlight Theatre, a favorite summertime treat for residents and visitors since 1951, hosts touring productions of Broadway musicals on a renovated 10-story state-of-the-art stage complex completed in 2000.

Events such as the Kansas City Blues & Jazz Festival and the 18th and Vine Heritage Jazz Festival draw local and national musicians and fans. The Kansas City Symphony, considered one of the finest regional symphonies in the nation, has built a sold-out following by taking classical music to the people. The Symphony performs at the Lyric Theatre and Yardley Hall in the Carlsen Center at Johnson County Community College, as well as offering more informal concerts in parks, hotel lobbies, and on museum lawns.

The Friends of Chamber Music has grown from a small group of friends to a powerful arts organization with a full season of world-renowned performers, ranging from quartets to large chamber orchestras. The Conservatory of Music at the University of Missouri-Kansas City originated in 1906 as a busy music school. Today, many fine musicians teach and train at the Conservatory, which offers more than 350 concerts and recitals by students and professionals each year in the Performing Arts Center on the university campus.

Kansas City is probably best known for its rich contribution to jazz. In the 1920s, '30s, and '40s, jazz greats such as Bennie Moten, Jay McShann, Lester Young, Charlie "Bird" Parker, Joe Turner, Count Basie, and Mary Lou Williams made Kansas City a special place. During the 1930s, Count Basie immortalized the area as "Twelfth Street and Vine." Now, Kansas City is also rediscovering its jazz heritage. Clubs and festivals create opportunities for the public to hear live jazz and for musicians from all over the country to meet and jam.

The Mutual Musicians Foundation, a national historic landmark at 1823 Highland, has been a jazz Mecca for more than fifty years. On weekends, musicians old and young get together for day and late-night jam sessions. Originally the Black Musicians Union Local 627, this organization has encouraged the careers of many jazz legends since its founding in 1904. Today, the Charlie Parker Memorial Foundation promotes the study of

music and dance by young black students, offering lessons on a sliding fee basis or by scholarship so that no aspiring youngster is turned away.

Indoors or out, Kansas City's theaters are plentiful and varied. With twelve professional theaters in operation, Kansas City is home to more professional theater companies than any city of comparable size in the United States, while ranking third in the nation for professional theaters per capita.

Since its debut as a university summer program in 1964, the Missouri Repertory Theatre has earned a national reputation by staging classics and contemporary plays and bringing actors and directors of national and international stature to Kansas City. The Rep has an excellent following all season, but during winter holidays, the annual production of Charles Dickens' *A Christmas Carol* is an especially well loved Kansas City tradition.

© Bruce Mathews, MIDWESTOCK

Buck O'Neil, one of Kansas City's best and most beloved ambassadors, visits the full-sized infield at the Negro Leagues Baseball Museum where he is immortalized in bronze along with other baseball greats.

The American Heartland Theatre emphasizes fun with comedies, musicals and murder mysteries. Located in Crown Center, the 420-seat theater is one of only two professional theater companies located in a retail center. The second, also located in Crown Center, is the Coterie Theatre, a professional theater for youth and family audiences with an emphasis on multi-cultural interests and regional reputation.

Smaller Equity and non-Equity companies are also thriving. The New Theatre in Overland Park is one of America's most successful dinner theaters, featuring nationally known guest artists.

Because of high New York production costs, small, regional theaters such as Kansas City's Unicorn Theater offer excellent opportunities to try out thought-provoking and sometimes controversial contemporary plays in an intimate setting.

The Heart of America Shakespeare Festival, founded in 1991, has rapidly grown into a much-anticipated annual event. The festival is free and entertains more than 245,000 people each summer with two alternating repertory performances of Shakespeare plays in the intimate setting of Kansas City's Southmoreland Park.

Classical to contemporary, traditional to experimental, sophisticated to folksy, Kansas City expresses its love of arts and culture in so many ways. Its love of art, theater, music, dance, history, and cultural heritage—like so many other facets of Kansas City life—is varied and diverse. ▨

"Kansas Citians are able to enjoy an ever-stronger, broad-based arts scene, the vibrancy of which reflects a vital and sustained partnership among our business and community leaders, local and regional arts organizations, and the talented and dedicated individuals who create and perform. Over the next several years, completion of new arts-related projects and initiatives will continue raising Kansas City's arts profile, both regionally and nationally."

Richard C. Green, Jr.
Chairman and Chief Executive Officer
UtiliCorp United

(Left)Named after wild berries that once grew here, Strawberry Hill Museum and Cultural Center in Kansas City, Kansas, sits atop the bluffs overlooking the confluence of the Kansas and Missouri rivers. The center houses arts and crafts and historical materials celebrating the Slavic roots of the area's residents.

(Following page) Reflections of Thomas Hart Benton's life are present in both his home and his paintings. A renowned painter, sculptor, lecturer, and writer, Benton had a gift for interpreting everyday life. Born in Neosho, Missouri, in 1889, Benton moved to Kansas City in 1939 after pursuing art instruction in Chicago and Paris, serving a brief stretch in the Navy and teaching in New York City. Benton's two-and-a-half story, late Victorian-style house is preserved as part of Missouri's Division of State Parks. Several of Benton's paintings and sculptures can be viewed in the house. Thomas Hart Benton died in his studio on Jan. 19, 1975, doing what he liked best—painting the American scene.

STRAWBERRY HILL
MUSEUM
AND
CULTURAL CENTER

OPENING
SAT. 12-5
SUN. 12-5

Photographic reproduction of Thmas Hart Benton artwork © Bruce Mathews, MIDWESTOCK

© Bruce Mathews, MIDWESTOCK

Whether attending a national debut of a contemporary ballet or the performance of the perennial regional favorite, The Nutcracker (right), dance lovers delight at the wide-ranging repertoires offered by the area's excellent dance companies.

Concerts, musicals, jazz sessions, and dance find many performance venues in Kansas City. Once the most elegant movie palace in the city, the 2,800-seat Midland Center for Performing Arts at 12th Street and Main hosts professional touring companies. Also a former movie house, the Uptown Theater at 37th Street and Broadway has been renovated and modernized for live concerts. Starlight Theatre in Swope Park seats nearly 8,000 people and is one of the best known open-air theaters in the nation.

© Jim Hays, MIDWESTOCK

© Bruce Mathews, MIDWESTOCK

TRUMAN HOUSE

Built about 1867 by George Porterfield
Gates, a mill owner. President Harry
S. Truman and his wife Bess Wallace
Truman, granddaughter of Gates, made
this their home from the time of
their marriage in 1919. The "Summer
White House" from 1945 to 1953.

Harry S. Truman, the 33rd President of the United States, made his home in this 14-room house in Independence, Missouri.

© Bruce Mathews, MIDWESTOCK

© Bruce Mathews, MIDWESTOCK

The Harry S. Truman Library and Museum serves as a historical museum and a research center, housing materials, papers, and artifacts from his administration.

© Bruce Mathews, MIDWESTOCK

The Johnson County Museum of History features a permanent exhibit, "Seeking the Good Life," about the post-World War II suburban boom. On the museum grounds is an original, completely restored all-electric home.

Kansas Citians fell in love with bovine art in the summer of 2001 when the Cows on Parade decorated street corners, parks, and sidewalks throughout the city. Here Charlie Parcow blows his sax outside the entrance to the Crown Center Shops.

The Avenue of the Arts along the side of Bartle Hall in downtown Kansas City serves as the foundation for the creation of a Performing Arts District featuring dining and entertainment venues with diverse attractions and public art.

© Kevin Sink, MIDWESTOCK

(Left) Sculptor Kenneth Snelson employed stainless steel cylinders to create Triple Crown, one of many original works commissioned by Hallmark Cards for Crown Center.

(Above) The Kemper Museum of Contemporary Art opened in 1994. The museum's exterior of concrete, glass, stainless steel, and granite often serves as a backdrop for outdoor sculpture.

8

Chapter Eight

LET'S PLAY!

Kansas City residents love the game—no matter what the game is. Rowing, rugby, baseball, or barbeque, Kansas Citians compete with all their hearts and strength.

© Kevin Sink, MIDWESTOCK

K ansas City is outdoor country where a "let's play" spirit sings throughout the region.

When it comes to sports, Greater Kansas City has something for every athlete and spectator, from the serious runner to the leisurely walker; from local fans to international superstars; from the sailor to the race-car driver; from peewees to senior athletes. Kansas Citians are dedicated to an energetic pursuit of athletics and recreation on every level for every individual.

A myriad of professional, collegiate, amateur, high school, youth, and recreational league sports teams call Kansas City home. They not only build the spirit and physique of area residents, but also propel the region's economy. Sports in Kansas City are more than just having fun—they are big business, pumping an estimated $750 million to $1 billion annually into the local marketplace. In fact, spectator sports draw more people per capita in Greater Kansas City than in any other major league city.

Pro teams

For the fan, Kansas City is a sports lover's paradise with NASCAR events, horse and dog racing, and six professional sports teams: Royals baseball, Chiefs football, Knights basketball, Attack indoor soccer, Wizards outdoor soccer,

Lakes and parks abound in Kansas City for outdoor recreation. Here Briarcliff Lake in the Northland enhances a surrounding upscale subdivision.

© Kevin Sink, MIDWESTOCK

and Explorers tennis. These clubs are not just Kansas City teams—they draw fans from states throughout the Midwest.

For forty years, professional football has been a passion for thousands who attend the Kansas City Chiefs games or watch the team's televised play. In 1962, Lamar Hunt moved his team, the Dallas Texans, to Kansas City. He renamed them the Kansas City Chiefs, in part to honor Mayor H. Roe Bartle, nicknamed "The Chief," who encouraged the move. The team, which had dominated the old American Football League, played in the first Super Bowl in January 1966, losing to the Green Bay Packers by a score of 35-10. Typical of the Kansas City spirit that overcomes defeat and discouragement, the Chiefs rallied to win the Super Bowl and the National Football League Championship in 1970.

Game day has taken on the air of a festival. Red shows up everywhere, in offices, in fountain lights, even on faces. Every season, 79,451 fans eagerly await the Chief's kickoff by tailgating outside Arrowhead Stadium. Arrowhead has been consistently recognized as one of the nation's top tailgating venues.

Arrowhead is part of the innovative Harry S. Truman Sports Complex on I-70, about eight miles east of Kansas City's downtown business district. The complex features the world's only side-by-side twin football/baseball stadiums. In addition to Arrowhead, the sports complex is the site of Ewing M. Kauffman Stadium, the 40,762-seat home of Kansas City's beloved Royals baseball team.

Kauffman Stadium is one of baseball's most splendid ballparks, with its 322-foot-wide water fountain that shoots triumphant home-run jets into the air; 12-story-high scoreboard; and 30-by-40-foot, color video board—the largest in the country—that instantly brings fans closer to important plays. The stadium opened in 1973 as Royals Stadium, but was renamed Kauffman Stadium in the summer of 1993 to honor owner and philanthropist Ewing Marion Kauffman, one of the city's most revered citizens.

Since coming to Kansas City in 1969, the Royals have won six American League Western Division Championships, two American League Pennants, and the 1985 World Series Championship. Recently, the Royals have averaged 1.6 million fans annually, and have one of the largest regional followings of any major-league franchise. Royals slugger George Brett, who spent his entire playing career with the Royals, was recently inducted into the Major League Baseball Hall of Fame and now works in the team's front office.

The Chiefs and Royals together bring more than $300 million annually into Kansas City's local economy, with $145 million of the total coming from out-of-town visitors.

The Kansas City Monarchs, a Negro League Baseball team, also called Kansas City home until the 1950s when it disbanded after baseball become integrated.

Fishing alone at Wyandotte County Lake or taking a walk with the family along a stream way trail, Kansas Citians enjoy the outdoors.

(Right) Kansas Speedway fans show their patriotism at the NASCAR Winston Cup Series Protection One 400 on September 30, 2001.

(Below) Visitors and local residents enjoy dining, gaming, and star-studded entertainment at the area's riverfront casinos.

© Photo by Tim Umphrey, Courtesy of Kansas Speedway

© David Morris, MIDWESTOCK

To honor the league's greats, Kansas City established the Negro Leagues Baseball Museum in the historic 18th & Vine District. The gallery is arranged on a time-line of African American and baseball history from the 1860s-1950s. The centerpiece is the "Field of Legends," which features twelve life-sized bronze cast sculptures of the most important players in Negro Leagues history.

The resurgence of the American Basketball Association in 2000 helped bring professional basketball back to Kansas City for the first time since 1985. The Knights currently play a 42-game schedule, with Kemper Arena serving as their home court.

Three professional soccer teams also call Kansas City home—the Spurs, the Wizards, and the Comets. The Comets captured the National Professional Soccer League Championship in 1993 and 1997. The Wizards won the Major League Soccer Championship in 2000.

With the first games in 1993, the Explorers are a franchise of the World Team Tennis League, and typically feature two male and two female world-ranked players. The team plays seven of their fourteen games in Kemper Arena.

The Woodlands, a $70-million track at 97th Street and Leavenworth Road in Kansas City, Kansas, is one of the nation's only dual racing facilities for dogs and horses. The site also hosts the annual running of The Woodlands Wiener Dog Nationals in July.

The $250 million Kansas Speedway opened in June 2001, bringing to the Midwest the increasingly popular sport of speed racing. The Speedway has seating for 75,000 with the possibility of expanding to 150,000. Unlike the area's other racing venues, I-70 Speedway, Lakeside Speedway and Kansas City International Raceway, the Kansas Speedway is equipped to host the increasingly popular NASCAR circuit.

College sports

With major universities in and near the region and more than two dozen colleges and community colleges, collegiate sports are also popular in Kansas City. The area is home to the University of Missouri-Kansas City Kangaroos, which entered Division 1 of the NCAA in 1987-1988, building on an already respectable record for the men and an impressive one for the women from years of National Association of Intercollegiate Athletics play. Big 12 sporting events are only a short drive away.

Leisure time and amateur sports

Kansas Citians find nearly unlimited amateur sports outlets in which to invest their leisure time, whether as a fan or an active participant. Amateur football has become such a part of the social life of the region that Friday nights in the fall are virtually monopolized by high-school games. Weekends and evenings are also filled with co-ed softball, Little League, swim meets, golf, basketball, and soccer for all ages. In addition, amateur softball, volleyball, handball, archery, yachting, sailing, hang-gliding, volleyball, lacrosse, field hockey, rugby, and even polo teams meet on organized playing fields throughout the region and flourish in parks, schools, and clubs both private and public. There are lanes for bowling, with an annual spring stop of the Professional Bowlers Association Tour.

Since it was introduced to the region in 1896, golf has captured the hearts of many Kansas Citians, as is evident in the growing number of courses—forty-one public, five semi-private, and twenty private courses—many of them championship quality. Renowned golf champion Tom Watson is a Kansas City native and helped design several area courses. Celebrity golf tournaments, including a stop on the Senior PGA Tour with the T.D. Waterhouse Championship, are important charity fundraisers.

Swope Park hosts the number-one folf (Frisbee golf) course out of 1,004 nationwide. The 18-hole professional folf course is the home of the U.S. Open Folf Tournament held annually in June. Rules of folf are similar to golf except that players throw Frisbees.

Once a country club sport, tennis is now widely popular in schools as well as parks and recreation programs throughout the area. Tennis players have their pick of more than 400 public and 100 private courts around the city, to work on their game. Serious young players compete in Missouri Valley-United States Tennis Association-sanctioned events.

Indoor and outdoor soccer remains popular for both competitive and recreational teams of all ages, including adult teams that are often coed. Recreational outdoor

© Bruce Mathews, MIDWESTOCK

soccer is one of the fastest growing sports among children in the metro. Indoor soccer has become so popular that area facilities schedule games from 6 a.m. through 1:30 a.m. the next morning.

Nearly year round, area rivers and lakes are filled with people enjoying their favorite water sports, such as swimming, boating, sailing, fishing, skiing, scuba diving, rowing, and white water rafting.

Water sports in Kansas City include the Kansas City Blazers, a team that trains swimmers from age 7 through their early 20s, including Olympic gold medalist Cathryn Fox. Competing at local, state, national, and Olympic levels, the Blazers are consistently ranked among the top ten teams at the United States Junior National events. The Kansas City Terrafins is a synchronized swimming team of women ages 15 to 18 who compete regionally and qualify for national events.

Outdoor enthusiasts take pleasure in a variety of fun— orienteering, sky diving, hot air balloon launches, skiing at nearby Snow Creek area in Weston, Missouri, or competitive bass fishing on one of the scores of lakes.

Kansas Citians also like running marathons to raise funds for charitable causes. The Hospital Hill Run is Kansas City's oldest running event and annually attracts nearly twenty-five hundred participants, including both local running enthusiasts and nationally ranked competitors, to test their stamina on the hilly terrain. *Runners' World* has ranked the half marathon as one of the nation's top 25 races.

Equestrian sports seem to go with the territory, partly because this is the home of the American Royal, the

With new links opening up each year, golf has remained a favorite sport in the region since 1896. Professional golfer Tom Watson—one of Kansas City's favorite hometown heroes— uses his talents in celebrity golf matches to raise funds for Children's Mercy Hospital.

© Bruce Mathews, MIDWESTOCK

Leisure time finds many outlets in the region—soaring through space in a hot air balloon, screaming on a Worlds of Fun roller coaster, dancing at the Kansas City Jazz Museum, or exploring at the Science City museum.

© Bruce Mathews, MIDWESTOCK

largest combined livestock exposition, horse show, and rodeo in the United States. Inaugurated in 1899, the Royal has become a Kansas City tradition that attracts owners and exhibitors from around the world showing 1,777 horses and 2,399 head of prime cattle annually.

Special Olympics

Nearly 2,800 athletes compete each year in the Kansas City Metro Special Olympics for children and adults with disabilities. With the help of 1,500 volunteers, these Olympians compete in a variety of sporting events, including alpine skiing, cross-country skiing, aquatics, basketball, bowling, cycling, figure skating, floor hockey, gymnastics, power lifting, roller skating, soccer, softball, tennis, and volleyball.

Headquarters for Associations

Many sports organizations have realized that Kansas City is located on the geographical "50-yard line" and "center court" of the rest of the country, offering an ideal location for their national headquarters. Those who have found homes in the Kansas City area include the National Association of Intercollegiate Athletics, the Fellowship of Christian Athletes, The Big Twelve Conference, the National Soccer Coaches Association of America (the largest single-sport coaching organization in the country), and the National Association of Basketball Coaches.

Parks

Kansas City, Missouri's Board of Parks and Recreation Commissioners oversee more than 9,100 acres of parkland in 201 parks, plus numerous fountains, community centers, golf courses, ball diamonds, pools, soccer fields, and tennis courts.

At 1,769 acres, Swope Park is the second largest urban park in the nation, ranking just behind New York's Central Park. It is home to the Kansas City Zoo and Lakeside Nature Center and hundreds of acres of picnic grounds, playing fields, hiking and biking trails.

Closer to the heart of town is the 75-acre Loose Park near the Country Club Plaza. The centerpiece is the Laura Conyers Smith Municipal Rose Garden, which has become a favorite spot for springtime weddings. Historical markers throughout the park provide information about the historic Civil War Battle of Westport.

A 650-mile Great Rivers corridor hike and bike trail system will eventually connect scores of cultural and historical centers throughout the metropolitan area. One of the first legs is the Heritage Trail, which features a mile-long lighted esplanade through Richard L. Berkley Riverfront Park, the only developed urban park on the banks of the Missouri River.

Southeast of the metro lies Powell Gardens, a not-for-profit botanical garden with 835 acres of rolling hills of fragrant, colorful gardens, native grasses, nature trails, wildflowers, and butterflies. The perennial garden is the largest in the Midwest, with more than 5,000 plants.

Also south of the city is the James A. Reed Memorial Wildlife Area near Lee's Summit, established in 1952 in memory U.S. Senator James A. Reed. The 2,456-acre wildlife area offers twelve lakes, ranging in size from one to forty-two acres and filled with largemouth bass, channel catfish, crappie, bluegill, sunfish and bullheads.

Burr Oak Woods Conservation Nature Center in Jackson County sits among forested land just twenty miles east of downtown Kansas City. The state park features 1,071 acres of woodlands, fields, and ponds and includes a scenic portion of Burr Oak Creek.

In Kansas, the 300-acre Overland Park and Botanical Garden is dedicated to the preservation of plant and wildlife indigenous to northeast Kansas. Relatively new to the area, the Arboretum with its children's garden and lengthy trail system has quickly earned the support of local residents and business community.

© Bruce Mathews, MIDWESTOCK

© Ben Weddle, MIDWESTOCK

Also in Johnson County is the 1,250-acre Shawnee Mission Park, the most visited park in the entire state of Kansas. It is one of three regional parks run by the Johnson County Parks and Recreation District, a National Gold Medal Winner for Park and Recreation Excellence. JCPR also oversees five thousand acres of parkland, including more than seventeen miles of continuous greenway trails along Mill Creek from Olathe to the Kansas River as part of a countywide Streamway parks system.

Wyandotte County, Kansas, has both the Missouri and Kansas Rivers running through and along its borders. Wyandotte County Lake and Park are the largest in the county.

Surrounding Kansas City are several other large lakes for sailing, fishing, skiing, and other water sports. North of the Missouri River is the 7,000-acre Smithville Lake and the smaller Weatherby Lake and Lake Waukomis. To the south, Jackson County Parks and Recreation's Lake Jacomo is a 970-acre lake located in the heart of Fleming Park. Colorful sailboat regattas, pontoon boat cookouts, and wave-runners are permanent fixtures in the warmer months. Nearby are Blue Springs Lake, also located in Fleming Park, and Longview Lake, part of the U.S. Army Corps of Engineers Little Blue River Project for flood control, recreation, and other water resource development.

Worlds of Fun

Worlds of Fun is a family theme park on 175 acres of land with 115 rides, shows, and attractions, including one of the world's tallest wooden roller coasters. The Mamba and Timberwolf are two of the top 25 roller coasters in the world, according to *Amusement Today*'s 2001 golden ticket awards. Its companion park, Oceans of Fun, is a water recreation park with a million-gallon wave pool, several water slides, various swimming pools, and 16 additional rides and shows.

In addition, many out-of-town visitors as well as local residents also enjoy dining, gaming, and star-studded entertainment at the area's riverfront casinos, such as The Isle of Capri, Harrah's North Kansas City, Argosy Casino, and Ameristar Casino Hotel. ◼

Tennis courts on the Country Club Plaza are among more than 500 public and private courts in the area.

Kansas City area residents play as hard as they work. Softball and baseball fields attract teams from spring through fall, and colleges recruit high school athletes who excel in their chosen sport. Many have gone on to compete in the Olympic games or professionally.

© Ben Weddle, MIDWESTOCK

"From baseball to basketball, football to soccer, Kansas City's sports tradition is legendary. Our professional and amateur athletes are committed to good sportsmanship and teamwork. Settling for second best isn't an option.

"We share that philosophy at Saint Luke's-Shawnee Mission Health System. We are dedicated to enhancing the physical, mental, and spiritual health of the communities we serve. We go beyond curing disease by helping our community prevent it. By working to keep Kansas City healthy, we all win."

G. Richard Hastings
President and Chief Executive Officer
Saint Luke's-Shawnee Mission
Health System

Kansas City is a major league city with major league fans who flock to the Harry S. Truman Sports Complex to tailgate before watching Kansas City Chiefs football action in Arrowhead Stadium, or Kansas City Royals baseball at Kauffman Stadium.

© John Mutrux, MIDWESTOCK

© Ben Weddle, MIDWESTOCK

© Bruce Mathews, MIDWESTOCK

Royals Hall of Fame slugger George Brett, far left, helped lead the team to win the World Series in 1985. All Kansas City celebrated with a ticker-tape parade for the team.

Located in the historic stockyards area of Kansas City, Kemper Arena plays host to many sporting events as well as musical concerts, three-ring circuses, and the nation's oldest and largest agricultural exhibition, the American Royal Livestock, Horseshow, and Rodeo.

© Kevin Sink, MIDWESTOCK

Photo by Ed Zurga, Courtesy of the Kansas City Wizards

Photo by G. Marc Benavidez / Kansas City Star

(Left) Midfielder Chris Klein celebrates his game-winning assist for the Wizards as they captured the 2000 Major League Soccer Cup Championship.

(Right) Kansas City Knight Guard Shea Seals goes up against Chicago Skyliner Antwon Hall during a Saturday afternoon game at Kemper Arena. Kemper also is host to the Kansas City Attack indoor soccer team.

Kansas City is world famous for its barbeque. Cook-offs, such as the annual Lenexa, Kansas, Barbeque Contest, determine the best sauces and techniques.

© Don Wolf, MIDWESTOCK

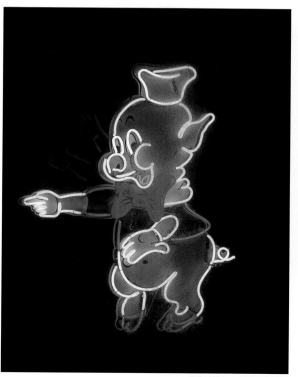

© David Morris, MIDWESTOCK

© Dewey Chapman, MIDWESTOCK

Everyone has a favorite restaurant—even a few U.S. Presidents who made it a point to grab a slab of ribs while in town.

© Jeff Morgan, MIDWESTOCK

*Kansas Citians enjoy
the outdoors through-
out the year, even in
winter when folks
slide across the ice at
Crown Center, or sled
down "suicide hill" in
Brookside.*

© Eric Berndt, MIDWESTOCK

On a quiet autumn morning, scores of sailboats rest on the placid water at Lake Jacomo in southern Jackson County, Missouri. © Kevin Sink, MIDWESTOCK

9

Chapter Nine

PROFITABLE PURSUITS

At the heart of America, Kansas City stands in the center of the nation, the center of transportation, and the center of commerce.

© Kevin Sink, MIDWESTOCK

Kansas City serves as a regional banking center since the establishment of a Federal Reserve Bank (below) here in 1914.

The Country Club Plaza (opposite) was developed by J.C. Nichols in the 1920s as the first outdoor shopping center catering to the automobile. The Plaza continues as a hub for retail, entertainment and professional services.

Greater Kansas City is good for business because Kansas City works. The facts are indisputable:

- Kansas City ranks among the top cities nationally in supporting small business and stands in ninth place among cities for entrepreneurial growth. It is recognized by a variety of sources as one of the best cities in which to start a business in today's market.
- Kansas City ranks in the top ten cities for transportation and distribution facilities.
- Kansas City claims the fastest growing job market in the Midwest.
- Kansas Citians historically get more done in less time than workers on either coast. Local production workers contribute 50 percent more value added per hour than the national average.
- Kansas City has the third healthiest work force in the nation. Area employees lose half as many work days to illness and injury as the national average.

- Kansas Citians are well educated. More than 90 percent of adults here have high school diplomas and more than one-third are college graduates, both achievements above the national average.
- Kansas City is the tenth most "wired" city in the United States with 61 percent of its residents on-line.
- Kansas City's central location and central time zone provide a longer workday window, making it a profitable home for transportation firms, major telemarketers, and other industries with a national reach.

The facts are that Greater Kansas City is a great place for commerce. Many Kansas City hometown companies appear on *Fortune Magazine*'s annual list of 500 top firms, including American Century Investments, Black & Veatch, Commerce Bancshares, DST Systems, Dunn Industries, Farmland Industries, H&R Block, Hallmark Cards, Interstate Bakeries, Kansas City Southern Industries, Sprint, UMB Financial, Utilicorp, and Yellow Corp. A number of these and other major league corporations have recently announced plans to open new operations locally or expand existing facilities.

Part of what makes Kansas City so successful is location, location, location. At the geo-center of the United States, the city serves as a leading transportation hub. Kansas City is one of only five cities in the nation to have three intersecting interstate highways that also carry international trade between Mexico and Canada. It is the second busiest rail center in the United States with four class I rail carriers and three regional railroads. Not only does Kansas City International Airport serve as a global port, there are eight regional airports in the metropolitan area, four of which receive large cargo airplanes. The Port of Kansas City is one of the nation's inland ports and is the largest storage and distribution center on the Missouri River. It, and a new port location at the former Richards Gebauer airport, are true intermodal facilities, transferring goods between barge, train, and truck.

Around the world, Kansas City also is being recognized as a growing hub for technology. The area claims a host of high-tech companies, workers, and support organizations, such as the industry leader in Global Positioning Systems technology and innovation, Garmin International, headquartered in Olathe; DST Systems, a home-grown world-class provider of financial, telecommunications, and video services; and Cerner Corporation, a major provider of software for the health care industry.

This high-tech bent makes Kansas City particularly attractive for any technology based idea, enterprise, or investor. Sixty percent of the area's fastest growing companies provide products and services to the technology industry, including biotechnology, computer networking, software development, information technology staffing, training, and consulting; hardware manufacturing, Web

© Kevin Sink, MIDWESTOCK

Formally chartered in 1876, the Kansas City Board of Trade is located in the heart of one of the most productive wheat growing regions of the world. Buyers and sellers engage in intense trading of commodities. In addition, Kansas City is a regional center for banking, financial services, and insurance.

© Michael Rush, MIDWESTOCK

hosting, and tech communications. Fifty-four of every one thousand private sector workers are employed by high-tech firms, ranking the area third among Midwestern cities in high tech employment.

Gaining and maintaining this reputation as a high-tech center has not happened overnight, but is the product of cooperative strategies on many fronts. In education, Kansas City has one of the largest privately endowed scientific and technological libraries in the Linda Hall Library of Science and Technology. The Center for Telecomputing Research at the University of Missouri-Kansas City is one of the premier centers for telecommunications and computer networking research.

One of the nation's leading independent research organizations, Midwest Research Institute, was established here in 1944 and has grown into an international center for applied research and technological development for government, business and industry.

Another partner in the cutting-edge technology arena is KCCatalyst, an area-wide organization dedicated to igniting the technology-based economic sector of the bi-state region. KCCatalyst links new technology companies with resources and expertise in established businesses and organizations. KCCatalyst works with groups such as the Greater Kansas City Chamber of Commerce, the Kansas City Area Development Council, the New

Economy Council of Greater Kansas City, and KTEC (Kansas Technology Enterprise Corporation).

KTEC itself has provided a true guidebook for those embarking on a technology venture. The KTEC network supports businesses, inventors, researchers, and entrepreneurs through each phase of the technology life cycle, from idea to product.

One of the most dynamic and promising technology adventures for the region is in life sciences. Civic and business leaders, scientists, and researchers want to fashion Greater Kansas City into a world center for life sciences research and development. In 2001, the Stowers Institute for Medical Research opened, a $195 million state-of-the-art center for the world's top life science researchers. Stowers has linked with several educational institutions of higher learning as well as MRI in providing facilities, sharing information and findings, and offering support services for this research.

Leading the life sciences strategy is Kansas City Area Life Sciences Institute, Inc., a not-for-profit umbrella organization dedicated to accelerating Kansas City into the lead position in the life sciences industry. The life sciences initiative focuses on research and development particularly in the specialties of cancer, cardiovascular disease, human development and aging, infectious diseases, and neurological diseases. Leaders in both Kansas

and Missouri are working together to create an economic and scientific environment to recruit top-flight researchers and biotech businesses to the area.

The Life Sciences Institute plans for the life sciences industry to become one of Kansas City's giant economic engines. The initiative aims at technology and information transfer into industry and consumer products for the medical breakthroughs that will come from the research. These discoveries will create new companies with new products and new jobs. Within ten years, the life sciences sector is projected to create fifteen thousand new jobs, increase the annual gross income in the metro by $650 million, and increase gross sales in the region by $1.1 billion. Venture capital firms already have invested hundreds of millions of dollars into Kansas City area technology and biomedical start-ups and are preparing to do even more.

Even so, Kansas City is far from a one-horse town. Its economic strength and stability rely on the diversification of its economic base. No one industry or one sector dominates the region's economy. Historically, this diverse economy buffered the area from the worst effects of major recessions and even the Great Depression. The high-tech sector is only one among many successful economic directions in Kansas City, which thrives with such varied fields as aviation, agribusiness, animal sciences, automotive, banking and financial services, insurance,

defense systems, retail sales, wholesale distribution, and communications.

Kansas City is a focal point for the telecommunications industry and back-office business. One of the area's largest private employers, telecommunications giant Sprint and Sprint PCS in Overland Park, has about eighteen thousand workers locally who are a part of an 84,000-person workforce worldwide. Southwestern Bell, AT&T, and other communications firms also have substantial operations here.

Greater Kansas City is also a major government center for the region, with the federal government claiming title as the area's single largest employer in both the public and private sectors. Located in the metropolitan region are offices of the Federal Aviation Administration, Small Business Administration, General Services Administration, Environmental Protection Agency, Internal Revenue Service, National Labor Relations Board, Departments of Agriculture, Commerce, Health and Human Services, Housing and Urban Development, Labor, and Transportation; and the U.S. Army Corps of Engineers District Office.

The 12th District Federal Reserve Bank, located since 1914 in Kansas City, serves banks in seven Midwest states. It is one of only two sites to print savings bonds in the United States.

Although the service sector is the fastest growing component of the local economic base, particularly in the

area of information technology, manufacturing continues as a strong segment. Among the manufacturers are two auto assembly plants—Kansas City ranks sixth in the nation in auto assembly—a motorcycle assembly plant, a steel mill, a pharmaceutical manufacturer, the nation's largest producer of greeting cards, a defense contractor, and an aircraft landing systems maker.

Of course, agribusiness remains a perennial Kansas City economic driver. Far from the down-on-the-farm small business, agriculture and animal health are sophisticated industries with research and development, manufacturing, marketing, sales, and distribution components located here. The country's largest farm cooperative, Farmland Industries, calls Kansas City home for its fifteen hundred farmer-owners in twenty-two Midwestern states. The Kansas City Board of Trade, established in 1886, is the country's leader in hard winter wheat marketing. The area ranks second nationally in wheat flour production, and third in grain elevator storage capacity. Its Value Line Index applies the principles of commodities investing to the stock market.

© Don Wolf, MIDWESTOCK

© Mark E. Gibson, MIDWESTOCK

Across the economic spectrum, Kansas City ranks first nationally in several other areas, including inland foreign trade zone space, frozen food storage and distribution, manufacturing instrument landing systems, and underground storage space.

In addition to its thriving business climate, Kansas City also holds a superb status for its quality of life. Kansas, for example, ranks sixth in the nation for overall quality of life and the bistate region received a five-star quality of life rating from a national magazine survey of 329 metro areas. Overland Park stands among the top ten cities in the nation for women in terms of quality of life and business opportunities and has been named the "kid-friendliest" city among large suburban communities in the nation. In addition, Kansas City has lower business and lifestyle costs than most major metropolitan areas and citizens enjoy an overall lower tax burden than the national average.

Contributing to the quality of life indicators is Kansas City's vibrant real estate market. The area stands in the top twenty-five hottest real estate markets in terms of costs and availability of downtown office space, suburban office space, and warehouse space. Based on price and availability in a range of housing categories, the Kansas City area is also in the top 10 percent of U.S. real estate markets and consistently ranks among the nation's most affordable housing markets. Families earning the local median income of $57,700 could afford to buy more than 80 percent of the houses sold in 2000. By comparison, in a city such as San Francisco, families earning the median income of $74,900 were able to afford only 6 percent of the homes for sale.

At the core of Kansas City's success story are its people. They are what make Kansas City businesses and industries stand out over those in other metropolitan areas.

© Michael P. Manheim, MIDWESTOCK

Although the citizens come from a wide range of ethnic groups and backgrounds, they share many attributes that contribute to business excellence. They are educated, hard working, rugged individualists who care about the welfare of their community. They are full of courage and stamina, good will and compassion, pride in their work, and are selfless in their generosity. They treat each other with respect, share their good fortune, and give back to the community that gave them a leg up in the first place. Kansas Citians have the imagination, savvy, muscle, and, most of all, the heart to get the job done, not just somehow, but to get the job done well. ▨

© John Borge, MIDWESTOCK

Kansas City is recognized internationally as a center for technology, including biotechnology, fiber optics, wireless communications, and computer software and hardware development and manufacturing.

Automation
Area
Keep Out

The General Motors Fairfax assembly plant, in Kansas City, Kansas, is one of the area's largest employers.

Manufacturing jobs are part of the healthy mix of businesses that keeps the region economically stable and strong.

"Charles Darwin is often misquoted as saying 'only the strongest survive.' What Darwin actually said is that it's not the strongest of the species that will survive, or the most intelligent. It's the ones who are most responsive to change. The Kansas City area business community—like Yellow Corporation—knows that change is the only real constant. We don't just accept it. We thrive on it."

Bill Zollars
Chairman, President, and CEO
Yellow Corporation

Kansas City's central location makes it a natural for transportation enterprises. The area is the second largest rail hub in the nation. Goods are shipped by rail, truck, air and barge, with connections worldwide.

© David Morris, MIDWESTOCK

© Patti McConville, MIDWESTOCK

© Bruce Mathews, MIDWESTOCK

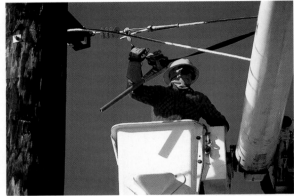

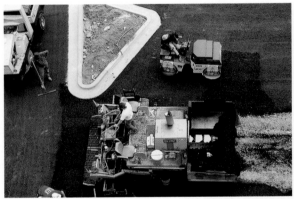

Kansas City's construction industry works almost year round to build homes, offices, retail centers, electric power plants, roads, sewers—all the structures and infrastructure that keep the city going and growing.

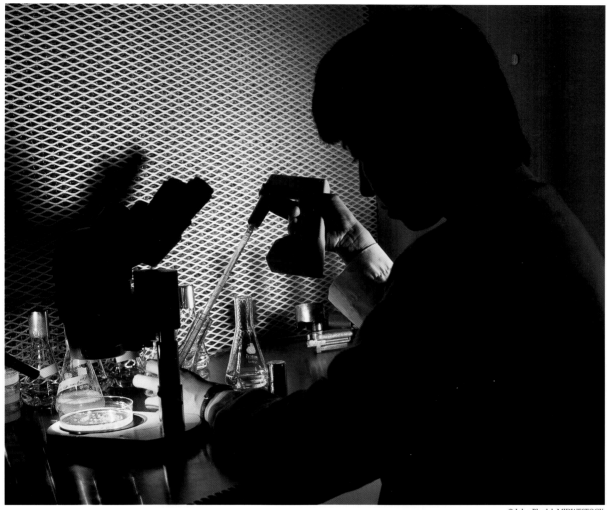

Agribusiness forms one of Kansas City's largest industries touching a long chain of consumers from the farmer, to the university professor, to the laboratory researcher, to the veterinarian and the grocery store shopper.

© John Blasdel, MIDWESTOCK

© Bruce Mathews, MIDWESTOCK

© John Blasdel, MIDWESTOCK

Kansas City's finest—firefighters and law enforcement officers—make it their job to keep businesses and homes safe. Near the Firefighters Fountain at 31st Street and Broadway is a memorial honoring all those who lost their lives battling fires since 1889.

© Susan Pfannmuller, MIDWESTOCK

© Jim Hays, MIDWESTOCK

© Eric R. Berndt, MIDWESTOCK

Part Two

10

Chapter Ten

BUSINESS, FINANCE &
THE PROFESSIONS

American Century Investments

I n the late 1950s, Twentieth Century Investors (now American Century) started out as one man, a metal desk, and a filing cabinet. Jim Stowers Jr. launched the company in his own apartment, where he balanced the books on one knee and his daughter on the other.

American Century's main office is located at 4500 Main Street, near the Country Club Plaza.

The early years were slow going. In fact, when one of the company's first employees found the bottom line at the end of 1965, he was so excited, he shouted: "We made $1,000! We made $1,000!"

But through the bleak years, through the worries about paying the bills on time, making a profit, and keeping the files off the floor (the basement office flooded every time it rained), Stowers kept his eye on his goal: to help people achieve their dreams.

"My reason for establishing this company was very simple," says Stowers, now chairman. "I wanted to help people become financially independent—to help them improve their lives and be able to do what they wanted to do, when they wanted to do it—through investing. That has remained my first and most important goal over the years."

That approach has paid off. Today, American Century's team of more than 250 investment professionals manages more than $85 billion in assets. Some 2 million investors— along with a who's who list of U.S. corporations, institutions, universities, and hospitals—look to American Century for investment management.

Helping People Achieve Dreams

On October 31, 1958, Twentieth Century offered the first shares of its flagship funds: Twentieth Century Growth Investors and Income Investors (now Select). Both funds focused on companies with accelerating growth. By the end of the year, the company had $405,164 invested.

From those modest beginnings has sprung a successful family of approximately 70 funds. Along the way, American Century has moved beyond its successful domestic growth investment process into other investment disciplines, including domestic and international growth equities, fixed income, quantitative and value-oriented equities, and global trading. And the investment management company also has expanded its offerings to include a variety of products and services for both individual and institutional investors.

Two partnerships have contributed to the company's growth and diversification. In 1995, Twentieth Century and The Benham Group, a mutual fund company known for fixed-income and money-market funds, joined forces to offer a full spectrum of funds. And in 1998, J. P. Morgan (now J. P. Morgan Chase & Company) purchased 45 percent of American Century, forming a business partnership focused on pursuing growth opportunities in asset management and personal financial services.

But more than 40 years after the company first offered its shares, one thing hasn't changed. Helping people improve their lives remains the bottom line for American Century.

American Century helped pioneer the use of computers in investment management in the early 1970s.

"Although we're a premier investment management company, we're not just in the numbers business," says Bill Lyons, American Century president and CEO.

"We are in the business of helping people. Our work can influence whether someone's child attends college or whether a couple retires comfortably. Two million people have entrusted us not just with their investments, but with their futures. That's why our vision doesn't talk about investment results; at the very top it says we're here to 'help people achieve their dreams.'"

Technology Trailblazer

American Century has long been a technology trail-blazer, having helped pioneer the use of computers in investment management in the early 1970s.

At the time, founder Jim Stowers Jr. was performing vigilant stock analysis through the time-consuming, laborious process of filling out forms by hand. After wearing out two Hewlett-Packard calculators, he leased an IBM computer, taught himself COBOL, and wrote a software program that calculated earnings and profits acceleration on 400 companies a day.

Today, the company continues to blaze a trail for the use of high-tech tools in investment management.

At American Century's Web site, *www.americancentury.com*, customers can do everything from open an account to make purchases to chat real-time with customer service—even redeem shares—24 hours a day, 7 days a week, via their own PCs. The result: some 80 percent of American Century's customer interactions occur online.

"By marshalling the power of technology, we can give investors greater convenience, control, and flexibility," says David McCalley, vice president of electronic commerce. "Investors can manage accounts with almost all the same services and transactions previously available only by phone, mail, or in person."

Investing in the Community

American Century's success has paid dividends for Kansas City as well, as the company has developed a reputation for investing in the community.

American Century's Mutual Friends program, for example, encourages volunteerism. In 2000, employees volunteered some 10,000 hours of service to organizations like United Way, Junior Achievement, and Habitat for Humanity. And the company puts its money where its mouth is, giving employees' favorite charities $200 to reward staffers for volunteering.

The company also supports the arts in Kansas City, sponsoring everything from the Heart of America Shakespeare Festival to the Plaza Art Fair to the Kansas City Symphony. American Century even commissioned world-renowned composer Rob Kapilow to write a symphonic piece to celebrate the city's 150th birthday.

Whether they call a toll-free number, visit an investor center, or download information from its Web site, American Century shareholders have always counted on easy access to products and services.

C. Kim Goodwin, chief investment officer, U.S. Growth Equities, has appeared regularly as a panelist on "Wall Street Week With Louis Rukeyser" since 1999.

Top: Sponsoring the Heart of America Shakespeare Festival is just one way American Century enhances the quality of life for the people of Kansas City. Right: American Century's generous employee benefits include free use of fully equipped on-site fitness centers.

To educate future investors, American Century helped develop Tips for Kids℠, a personal finance and investment curriculum for middle-school students. In this program, pre-teens learn the history of money, the benefits of investing early—even how to assemble a business plan. The program has gained national attention and now supports teachers in all 50 states, plus six other countries.

Through corporate philanthropy, the company quietly supports more than 85 local agencies, donating approximately one percent of net profits to the communities in which its people work.

But perhaps the most impressive example of American Century's influence on Kansas City is the Stowers Institute, a gift of founder and chairman Jim Stowers and his wife, Virginia.

Best Place to Work

American Century believes in sharing its success with the employees who contributed to its performance. For example, when American Century dramatically exceeded its goals in 1999, the company celebrated by handing each employee an extra paycheck. When the company achieved an important asset milestone in 2000, employees attended a blowout party featuring singing and dancing by '70s-costumed executives. Company leaders are known for grilling hamburgers or flipping pancakes to feed hard-working employees during crunch times.

With a culture like that, no wonder American Century has been recognized as one of the best places in America to work by *Fortune* and *Working Mother* magazines. Among other things, the publications cited the company's:
- Commitment to developing its people; it generally fills more than 50 percent of all job openings with internal staff;
- Innovative and generous benefits, such as its one-month sabbatical and a health plan that employees can apply to any household member—a sibling, parent, or even nanny; and
- Unique perks, such as a LifeCycle Account that pays for self-improvement of many kinds, from guitar lessons to ski-lift tickets to digital cameras.

"We're known as a company that searches for the best people," says Jerry Bartlett, chief people officer. "We seek people who are talented, resourceful, and dedicated, and then provide an environment where they can excel."

An American Success Story

American Century's is a culture focused on helping— the investor, the employee, the community. Since 1957, that approach has made American Century an American success story.

As Stowers likes to say: "I have always believed that if I help people become successful, they, in turn, will help me become successful." 🔷

Stowers Institute for Medical Research

The Stowers Institute for Medical Research, a state-of-the-art basic research facility, is the outgrowth of the wealth generated by American Century Investments and the generosity of Jim and Virginia Stowers. Seldom has there been a more direct link between the modest startup of a business—more than 40 years ago—and a major philanthropic endeavor.

Situated on a 10-acre campus in the heart of Kansas City, the Stowers Institute for Medical Research seeks to become one of the word's most innovative biomedical research institutions.

Photo by Mike Sinclair

When Jim Stowers talks about why he and Virginia have poured their fortune into the creation of the Stowers Institute he will inevitably say that they are giving back something "more valuable than money" to the millions of investors in American Century mutual funds who made their success possible. That valuable asset is Hope for Life®, not only for the American Century investors and their descendants but all of humanity.

Demonstrating in a spectacular way their commitment to foster great scientific research at the Stowers Institute and in the Kansas City area, Jim and Virginia Stowers have contributed almost the entirety of an endowment worth more than $1.6 billion to support the work of the Institute.

"Everything we are doing is focused on the goal of making this Institute the best of its kind within 25 years," Stowers said when the largest part of their gift, $1.114 billion in American Century stock, was announced in May 2001. "It is the centerpiece of our dream of making the Kansas City area into a 'Biomed Valley' that will lead the world in biomedical research."

The Stowers Institute, occupying a 10-acre campus in the heart of Kansas City, has 600,000 square feet of laboratory, office, and support space built at a cost of more than

$200 million. The first four scientific teams, each made up of five to ten people, moved into their laboratories in November 2000. In the summer of 2001, six additional lead scientists were recruited, plus two highly ranked experts in bioinformatics and transgenic technology.

By 2004, the Institute is likely to be completely filled, with about 600 people, including 40 to 50 independent research teams.

Jim and Virginia Stowers are both cancer survivors, and that experience shaped their decision to put the fruit of their labor behind research. They concluded that the best possibilities in achieving eventual breakthroughs in medical treatment lay in basic research focused on understanding the genes and proteins that control the behavior of cells in our bodies. By understanding these fundamental processes, scientists believe they can discover how diseases with genetic links occur, including cancer, Parkinson's, and dementia.

Each research team is led by a senior scientist with a distinguished record of research and publication or an assistant scientist who has done notable work at the postdoctoral level. Dr. Robb Krumlauf serves as scientific director, coming from England's National Institute for Medical Research at Mill Hill, London.

Dr. William B. Neaves, who joined the Institute in June 2000 as president and CEO, coming from the University of Texas Southwestern Medical Center at Dallas, has moved recruitment forward at a rapid pace. All of the lab leaders are selected with the approval of an advisory body made up of five members of the National Academy of Sciences.

Ever the capitalist dreamers, Jim and Virginia Stowers have continuously looked for ways to leverage their gift for the benefit of humanity and their community. They want to bring about cutting-edge research that will, in turn, help to catalyze further research in the academic and research institutions of the Kansas City metropolitan area and throughout the surrounding states of Kansas and Missouri. They are inspiring others to join them in dreaming big. ▓ *This page sponsored by American Century.*

Stowers Assistant Scientist Dr. Ting Xie is one of 10 independent scientists who lead research teams at the institute and is also the institute's first recipient of a National Institutes of Health grant resulting from a new research proposal submitted by the Stowers Institute. Photo by Don Ipock

State Street

From a landmark office tower on Quality Hill, the 1,000-plus Kansas City employees of State Street can see where it all began—the confluence of the Kaw and Missouri rivers, where French trappers established a settlement in 1821.

These days, the Kansas City economy depends more on financial services than on furs. Goods are delivered via web technology, not raft. And among today's mainstays of Kansas City business stands State Street, one of the world's leading specialists in serving the needs of sophisticated investors.

"For Everything You Invest In" is State Street's motto, and since the company was founded in 1792 as the Union Bank in Boston, State Street has grown to be a world leader in serving the needs of investors, with more than $5.8 trillion in assets under custody and $703 billion under management.

With offices in 23 countries, State Street serves more than 2,000 organizations and millions of individuals through its investment management business. State Street is the number one servicer of U.S. mutual funds, the number one custodian of mutual funds, number one as a servicer and investment manager for U.S. pension plans, and the number six investment manager worldwide.

State Street is dedicated to helping clients succeed in meeting their investment goals—a mindset that has driven the Kansas City office since it was established in 1972. Founded as Investors Fiduciary Trust Company by two other iconic local companies, Kansas City Southern Industries and DST Systems, IFTC was acquired by State Street in 1995 and took on the parent company's name in 1999.

State Street's Kansas City location has doubled in size in recent years, which has been good news for the Kansas City community as well as for the economy. State Street not only encourages business growth, but also empowers employees to serve as volunteers in support of charitable organizations. The company formed a community support program (CSP) in 1995 to support and amplify the volunteer efforts of its employees. Through CSP, grants are distributed to local charities to address education, health, housing and community development, and human survival. In recent years, State Street has provided grants to agencies including The Folly Theatre, Science City, Junior Achievement, The Salvation Army, the American Cancer Society, and many others.

In a dramatic display of State Street's commitment to Kansas City, the company celebrated the year 2000 with a Millennium Gift of $250,000 to the Kansas City chapter of Habitat for Humanity, making it possible to build new homes for low-income families— almost an entire city block's worth.

On the average each employee donates one day a year to helping others in Kansas City, whether it be running in a race to raise donations, hammering nails to help construct a playground, or volunteering at other charitable events.

State Street's 1,000-plus Kansas City employees enjoy the urban setting of the company's offices downtown.

Overlooking the heart of Kansas City, State Street's offices combine state-of-the-art technology with wonderful views from atop the limestone bluffs where the company has helped restore the historic Quality Hill district to its 19th century bustle.

State Street also supports the United Way throughout North America with both corporate and employee contributions. Each year, Kansas City employees exceed their goal for supporting more than 150 nonprofit agencies in the Kansas City area.

State Street employees serving as mentors at Central High School in Kansas City has proven to be a valuable partnership for students and mentors alike. Students are exposed to various areas of the company from Information Technology applications to mock interview sessions.

State Street maintains an Internet presence with the hope of facilitating communications within the community as well as with its employees. This emphasis on technology is keeping with State Street's position as an investment technology, information, and knowledge company. How important is technology in serving clients' needs? State Street commits about 20 percent of its operating expense budget to technology and technologists.

For more information on State Street's Kansas City office, please visit *www.statestreetkc.com*.

$\mathcal{KPMG\ LLP}$

$\mathbf{K}$PMG LLP in Kansas City has a future that is bright and growing. While many other accounting and tax firms are closing offices around the nation, KPMG is the fastest growing "Big 5" firm. KPMG is known worldwide for devising results-oriented business strategies, providing insights that help its clients stay ahead of the competition and achieving market-leading results.

The Kansas City office is one of 145 offices in the United States. The Kansas City office employs more than 160 employees in the downtown area and consistently is ranked as one of the top accounting and tax firms by the *Kansas City Business Journal*. KPMG is a U.S. member firm of KPMG International. KMPG International's member firms have more than 103,000 professionals, including 6,500 partners, in 152 countries. Total revenues equal $13.5 billion.

KMPG's Kansas City office opened in downtown in 1908. Prior to becoming KPMG LLP, the firm was known as Peat Marwick. Two Scottish immigrants, James Marwick and S. Roger Mitchell founded Marwick, Mitchell & Co. in New York in 1897. In 1924, the company merged with William Peat's British accounting firm, which established it as an international partnership. Finally, in 1987, Peat Marwick International merged with Klynveld Main Goerdeler to form Klynveld Peat Marwick Goerdeler (KPMG).

In Kansas City, KPMG serves clients within five lines of business: Consumer Markets, Financial Services, Industrial Markets, Information, Communication & Entertainment, and the Health Care & Public Sector.

• Consumer Markets: KPMG serves a broad range of clients that either make or sell consumer products, from household name manufacturers and retailers to private-line producers of food, home furnishings, fashion and apparel, cosmetics, and other personal care products.

Providing sound advice and innovative ideas to Kansas City's largest companies has always been a cornerstone of KPMG's success; here, partners confer at a strategy meeting about solutions to their clients' needs.

- Financial Services: In this industry, KPMG serves clients with issues encompassing banking and finance, insurance, and real estate concerns.
- Industrial Markets: In this line of business, KPMG serves four sectors—Chemicals & Pharmaceuticals, Energy & Natural Resources, Industrial & Automotive Products, and Transportation.
- Information, Communication & Entertainment: KPMG serves clients in the converging fields of Electronics, Software, Communications, and Media.
- Health Care & Public Sector: This includes federal and state agencies, cities, counties, financing authorities, hospitals, health-care systems, managed care organizations, universities, public benefit corporations, foundations, and other organizations that serve the public.

Relationships with existing clients are stronger than ever, and KPMG continues to win new opportunities at a rapid pace. That is why KPMG feels strongly about giving back to the community of Kansas City, whether it be a financial donation or a donation of in-kind services. KPMG is proud to have been involved in the following community redevelopment projects: Quality Hill, River Market, and Union Station.

Currently, 10,000 people live in downtown Kansas City. These numbers rose one-third in the 1990s and are projected to keep growing. Because of this, these three re-development projects are important to the growth of downtown Kansas City. The redevelopment projects will bring new properties—apartments, town houses, lofts, and historic houses—to the Downtown River Market, Quality Hill, and Union Station neighborhoods.

Employee volunteers have provided several Kansas City area charitable organizations much needed assistance through KPMG's INVOLVE Program.

Through one of KPMG's major internal programs— the INVOLVE Program—members of KPMG are encouraged to participate in various volunteer programs in the community. Programs include Habitat for Humanity, March of Dimes, United Way, American Red Cross, Juvenile Diabetes Foundation, and the company's charitable contributions program.

People in KPMG's local office are used to seeing a Kansas City influence in the firm's executive suite. Stephen Butler, current KPMG chairman and CEO, is the second of the past three firm chairmen to have worked in the Kansas City office. Larry Horner, former managing partner of the Kansas City office, was chairman from 1984 to 1990. Another former KC managing partner, Don Sloan, served as Peat Marwick's deputy chairman from 1978 through 1984. This speaks volumes to the caliber of professionals that practice in the Kansas City office.

KPMG has more than 100 years of experience in the health-care industry and is dedicated to addressing the needs of health-care providers, payors, suppliers, and the emerging intermediaries that are helping to transform the industry. KPMG is a frequent sponsor and participant in numerous industry programs and conferences. ▓

Recognizing the accomplishments of individuals in the organization is a core value at KPMG; applauding employee achievements is commonplace at Kansas City's staff meetings.

Greater Kansas City Chamber of Commerce

The Greater Kansas City Chamber of Commerce is the region's oldest business organization, and the only one serving both sides of the state line.

Founded in 1887, The Chamber has worked for the continuous improvement of the area's business environment. Many of the issues at the top of The Chamber's agenda are still at the top of the list today—issues such as infrastructure, economic development, international trade, and more.

In the early days, Chamber leaders tackled the city's infrastructure, lobbying the state legislature to form parks and municipal water works and to attract new manufacturers to the area. These leaders worked on bond issues to build a City Hall, sewers, and new schools, and promoted business relations with Mexico. Supporting development of the downtown business district, many of the city's now-historic buildings were built from the 1920s to 1940s including Union Station and Municipal Auditorium.

During World War II, Kansas City, with the support of The Chamber, created the Midwest Industrial Council to bring wartime jobs to Kansas City. The Midwest Research Institute was created to spur the development of technology in the Kansas City area and throughout the Midwest. A bond issue was passed for construction of the Starlight Theatre, Southwest Trafficway and 6th

Small business is a big deal at The Chamber, where more than 95 percent of our membership is made up of businesses with fewer than 250 employees. The Chamber honors ten of the metro area's brightest entrepreneurs at the annual Small Business Celebration, one of the largest events of its kind in the United States. © 2001 Bruce Mathews

Street Trafficway, as well as airport improvements. Since then, Kansas City has brought major league sports to town in the form of the National Football League's Kansas City Chiefs and Major League Baseball's Kansas City Royals. The city has grown through annexation efforts, and in the late '60s, a bond issue to construct Kansas City International Airport was successful.

The Greater Kansas City Chamber of Commerce continues to support the city's civic and business interests by serving as the "Champion of Business," promoting both small and large businesses.

All major private employers in the area are members of The Chamber, as are more than 2,200 small businesses. The Greater Kansas City Chamber of Commerce is the only bistate chamber serving businesses on both sides of the Missouri-Kansas state line and is the largest in Greater Kansas City.

The Chamber works for its members in a variety of ways to build a greater Kansas City and promote regional unity and growth. These efforts include: lobbying on business legislation in the state capitals of Missouri and Kansas, in Washington, D.C., and at Kansas City, Missouri, City Hall; enhancing growth and development of small business and entrepreneurship; expanding international trade; promoting the availability of a skilled and educated workforce; and encouraging activities to unite the two-state area.

The initiation of the first bistate cultural tax—a key priority for The Chamber—created the necessary funds to restore the city's historic Union Station. Many business people and families alike enjoy the multitude of activities from a hands-on Science City Museum to restaurants, shops, and theaters inside the newly-renovated landmark.

The POWER program, Partnering Organizations With Essential Resources, is a minority business development initiative started by The Chamber and our Minority Business Alliance partners in January 2000. The program includes monthly educational and networking sessions, and a mentoring component, and it continues to expand to include African-American, Hispanic and Latino, and Asian and American Indian-owned businesses. The first class of mentees is pictured here with Chamber leadership. © 2001 Bruce Mathews

The Kansas Citian of the Year award is the highest honor that The Chamber can bestow. Each year, at Annual Dinner, an individual is presented this award for civic contributions and achievements that have reflected the insight, creativity, and consciousness necessary to build and maintain a quality urban community. Past winners include, back row, left to right, Don Hall, Jack Steadman, Ollie Gates, and the Rev. Emanuel Cleaver II. In the front row, past winners Adele Hall, Bob Kipp, Anita Gorman, and Dick Berkley.

© 2001 Bruce Mathews

The Chamber is leading the charge in Kansas City to create SmartPort, an effort to make the area an inland trade port and bring together business interests in the United States, Canada, and Mexico. The purpose: open trade and commerce amongst members of the North American Free Trade Agreement (NAFTA).

The Chamber also sponsors GLOBE (Global Leadership Opportunities for Business Executives) to give members broad-based training in methods and practices of international business. This program is sponsored by The Chamber's World Trade Center. The Chamber's World Trade Center is one of 330 such centers around the world and is designed to promote international trade.

In addition, The Chamber is active in helping businesses recruit and retain employees. One resource for both employers and employees is a user-friendly online job board (*www.kchasjobs.com*). The Chamber's Workforce Solutions Program partners with a number of organizations to help promote a workforce that will meet industry needs. A five-industry consortia is working to help solve these workforce needs. Industries including hospitality/ entertainment/tourism, building and construction trades, health care, banking and finance, and information technology/telecommunications.

Efforts are ongoing to position Greater Kansas City both within the U.S. and internationally as the most recognized, premier location for research and development in the life sciences arena. Under the umbrella of the Kansas City Area Life Sciences Institute, Inc., lies an initiative to bolster local activity in every component of research, education, and industry that relates to human health care. By pooling fiscal resources to expand biomedical research and expanding research capabilities by sharing information between institutions, Kansas City has the potential to create up to 14,500 new jobs in research-related fields and produce an economic impact of $654 million over the next several years.

Being the "Champion of Business," The Chamber also advocates the interests of small businesses and entrepreneurs. Approximately 95 percent of The Chamber's membership is made up of small businesses with fewer than 250 employees. The organization strives to recognize and celebrate the efforts of the small business owner by recognizing the city's Top 10 Small Businesses at special events each year. Educational opportunities are available on topics such as: successful selling, marketing, and sound business practices.

Other benefits of Chamber membership include *Greater Kansas City Business*, a monthly magazine that spotlights members and shares success stories. Topics cover health, government, management, technology, workforce, marketing, and many other areas of interest to business owners. Visitors and members are welcome to browse through the entire contents of The Chamber's membership directory and buyer's guide online or check out The Chamber's Web site at *www.kcchamber.com*.

There's strength in our numbers at The Chamber, and nowhere is that more evident than in our government relations activities. Legislators regularly visit with members at meetings and receptions held at The Chamber, and each year a delegation of members and staff go to Washington D.C. to meet with legislators there.

Lathrop & Gage

Lathrop & Gage was named "Best Law Firm" in *Ingram's* magazine's "Best of Business Kansas City." According to the publication, the relationship between Kansas City and Lathrop & Gage is similar to the one that the firm shares with its clients: a rich history of growing and flourishing together through a continually changing business landscape.

As the third largest firm in Kansas City, Lathrop & Gage is a multi-disciplinary firm with more than 13 practice areas serving local, regional, national, and international clients from offices in Kansas City, St. Louis, Springfield, and Jefferson City, Missouri; Overland Park, Kansas; Boulder, Colorado; and Washington, D.C. Current clients include American Multi-Cinema, Inc., Bank of America, Bayer Corporation, Burlington Northern Santa Fe Railroad, Butler Manufacturing, Children's Mercy Hospital, General Motors Corporation, John Deere, Shawnee Mission School District, Sprint, and Tension Envelope to name a few.

With more than 400 employees, 225 of whom are attorneys, the firm's clients are allied with a group of attorneys possesing unparalleled expertise. Lathrop &

Lathrop & Gage values strong client relationships and holds a long-term view of the client alliance. Greg Williams, Legislative Aid to Kansas City, Missouri Mayor Barnes; Allison Bergman, firm attorney; Jerry Riffel, firm attorney; H. Darby Trotter, Ph.D., Vice President of Strategic Planning and Gordon Beaham, Chairman & CEO both of Faultless Starch-Bon Ami Company, pictured at a recent event. Photo by Mark McDonald

Gage's attorneys have either been recruited from top law schools across the country or have joined the practice after establishing a reputation for excellence in their area of expertise.

Changing Expectations

Lathrop & Gage changes client's expectations. Clients discover that working with the firm is a unique experience that goes above and beyond what they expect from a law firm. Lathrop & Gage attorneys have a long-term view of the client relationship and offer a complete sharing of information and resources. Attorneys and staff deliver legal services through creative problem solving after gaining a complete understanding of client needs. Lathrop & Gage offers the depth and strength of a national firm with the hands-on service, management style, and aggressive competition of a smaller firm.

A recent feature in *Of Counsel* magazine named Lathrop & Gage one of the legal industry's "best kept secrets." The publication—a practice management report published for corporate counsel—placed Lathrop & Gage

Lathrop & Gage is actively involved in the political and civic arena locally, regionally, and nationally. Terry Satterlee, firm attorney; Bert Bates, firm attorney; Missouri Senator Jean Carnahan; and David Shorr, firm attorney, pictured at a recent event. Photo by Mark McDonald

on its list of 40 "underrated" firms. Long-time Lathrop & Gage client Rufus Wallingford named the firm to this list based on "consistently high performance at very attractive rates."

A Rich History

Founded in 1873, Lathrop & Gage is the oldest law firm in continuous existence in Kansas City and is believed to hold this distinction for the western half of the United States. Maintaining long-term client relationships and providing cost-effective, top-quality service are the firm's guiding principles. Lathrop & Gage still represents its first client, Burlington Northern Santa Fe Railroad (known then as the Atchison, Topeka & Santa Fe Railroad Company). Many other clients have had relationships with the firm for well over a century.

Lathrop & Gage has played an important role in developing Kansas City. Between 1909 and 1914, the firm negotiated the Kansas City Terminal Railroad Company's franchise from the city, handling all the legal issues related to the acquisition of real estate and construction of Union Station. In the 1920s, the firm handled all details of the merger between Peet Brothers Manufacturing Co. and Colgate Palmolive Co. In the 1960s, Lathrop & Gage acted as legal counsel for several areas of Kansas City redevelopment, including Ten Main Center, Commerce Tower, Hallmark Cards' headquarters and development in Crown Center, and the expansion of Children's Mercy Hospital. Currently, Lathrop & Gage is legal counsel to the Kansas & Missouri Metropolitan Culture District Commission. This bi-state commission oversaw the tax that was used to restore and reconstruct the historic Union Station and Science City, a $256 million project.

Lathrop & Gage also plays an important role in the political arena. Members of the firm have served as United States senators, state governors, federal and state judges, city council members, and police commissioners and have provided professional and civic leadership as presidents of The Missouri Bar Association, The Kansas Bar Association, local bar associations in Missouri and Kansas including trial bars, and the University of Missouri Board of Curators. The firm's lawyers and staff also are active in local, state, and national politics and serve on or chair the boards of more than 100 local and regional charitable and civic organizations.

Vision for the Future

Lathrop & Gage continues to grow and expand across the country. In 2000, the firm merged with a firm in Springfield, Missouri to create one of the largest firms in southwest Missouri. In 2001, the firm added key attorneys in its St. Louis and Washington, D.C., offices to continue enhancing its government affairs practice. Lathrop & Gage recently opened a new office in Boulder, Colorado

Lathrop & Gage recently moved its Overland Park, Kansas office to a new building in Corporate Woods. As one of the largest law firms in Kansas, the expanded space will better accomodate the firm's growing client base in Johnson County. Tom Stewart, Managing Partner of Lathrop & Gage; Senator John Vratil, firm attorney; Kansas Governor Bill Graves; Kansas Lieutenant Governor Gary Sherrer; and Harry Wigner, firm attorney, celebrate the opening of their new facility. Photo by Mark McDonald

to serve that region's growing high-tech industry. Lathrop & Gage has developed one of the largest intellectual property and patent law practices in the Midwest, with more than 20 attorneys specializing in those high-demand practice areas.

One thing is clear—Lathrop & Gage will continue to grow in depth, breadth, and geographic scope. Most importantly, the firm will persevere in providing clients with services that reach above and beyond expectations. "We strive to know our clients and their businesses. We want to represent them in whatever direction they go," said Tom Stewart, managing partner of Lathrop & Gage.

H&R Block

With a new look, H&R Block enters the 21st century as more than the country's largest tax preparation firm. It is also becoming a financial partner to Mainstream America, offering financial services, products and home mortgages—year round.

For most people, tax time is the only time they take stock of their financial situation, and millions of taxpayers each year share the details of their situation with H&R Block. As a result, they think of Block as a financial services company and often ask for advice on financial planning.

"When our clients describe what they want from H&R Block, it's about helping them with many aspects of their financial lives, from saving for their future to buying a home," said Mark A. Ernst, H&R Block's president and chief executive officer. "Until now, many of them didn't feel they had an approachable company to turn to for financial advice."

H&R Block's clients receive financial and tax assistance practically anytime and anywhere they want through the company's expanded online services. mortgage assistance, brokerage services, annuities, mutual funds and IRAs—as well as tax preparation and filing services—are just a mouse click away.

Block is integrating its online capabilities with its retail tax office network to give clients the speed and convenience of the Internet with personalized tax advice that only Block can provide. So the do-it-yourself tax preparer never has to do it alone—Block is there to answer questions, review their work, or take over the entire preparation and provide a completed tax return—all online.

Findings from a recent Gallup survey echo what H&R Block is saying. Approximately 48 percent of the population doesn't have a financial plan, while nearly 70 percent believe they are not saving enough and are concerned about funding their retirement.

To communicate that the new H&R Block is now America's financial as well as tax partner, the company recently introduced its first logo redesign in more than two decades. A bright green block now signals an innovative and dynamic approach to serving its more than 22 million tax clients worldwide.

The new logo will be seen at the company's more than 10,400 tax offices located in the United States, Canada, Australia, and the United Kingdom, as well as 180 H&R Block Financial Centers coast to coast.

H&R Block's newly introduced logo signals its expansion into financial and mortgage services.

Mark Ernst, president and CEO, and Frank Salizzoni, chairman of the board, lay the groundwork for building a financial partnership with clients.

Brian DiGiorgio, vice president of the Service Center (standing), helps specialists answer client questions about financial services.

H&R Block was founded on Jan. 25, 1955, in Kansas City by brothers Henry and Richard Bloch. They changed the name to "Block" to make it easier for people to pronounce and spell. Tax preparation was offered for $5 back then, and the company was successful in its first year, resulting in expansion to New York in 1956. With more than 10,000 offices, H&R Block is the fourth largest retailer in the world. Its world headquarters is located at 4400 Main Street, just blocks away from the company's first tax office at Westport and Main streets.

"One of our biggest accomplishments was to legitimize the tax assistance industry by fighting for government regulation to protect the consumer," said Henry Bloch who retired in September 2000 as chairman of the board of directors. "I'm proud that we helped define a new industry that assists so many clients as they face the yearly challenge of complying with the tax laws.

"For years we've been the number one trusted advisor for Americans seeking assistance with their tax returns," he said. "Now, we are expanding our role into that of a financial advisor, giving people someone they can turn to for both their tax and financial needs. It's a natural evolution of our heritage." Y

Usage of H&R Block's four online tax services is monitored from the company's Kansas City data control center.

General Electric

General Electric (GE) brings good things to life in Kansas City. Three businesses with a major Kansas City presence are GE Employers Reinsurance Corporation, headquartered in Overland Park, Kansas; GE Card Services, located in Merriam, Kansas; and GE Transportation Systems Global Signaling, located in Blue Springs, Missouri.

With revenues of $130 billion in 2000, GE is a diversified technology services and manufacturing company with a commitment to achieving customer success. GE operates in more than 100 countries and employs 313,000 people worldwide.

Situated on a 27-acre campus in Overland Park, GE ERC is the world's fourth largest reinsurance company.

The company traces its beginnings to Thomas Edison. GE is the only company listed in the Dow Jones Industrial Index today that was part of the original index in 1896.

GE is recognized as a leader in every sense. FORTUNE magazine has described GE: "Tireless innovation. Robust financials. The ability to lure and keep the smartest people." According to FORTUNE, no company in the nation demonstrates such enviable qualities better than General Electric—putting GE atop the magazine's annual list of America's Most Admired Companies four years in a row.

Additionally, GE is committed to being a respected corporate citizen. Employees give more than one million hours of their time to volunteer initiatives. Collectively, the GE companies worldwide contribute more than $90 million annually to support education, the arts, the environment, and human service organizations.

GE Employers Reinsurance Corporation (GE ERC)

GE Employers Reinsurance Corporation (GE ERC) is a diverse reinsurance and commercial insurance business with deep Midwestern roots and vast global resources. The company's world headquarters is situated on a 27-acre corporate campus on Metcalf Avenue in Overland Park.

GE ERC sells insurance and risk transfer solutions to insurance companies, corporations, and professionals worldwide. GE ERC insures everything from the Sydney Opera House to Italian soccer teams to family physicians.

GE ERC is one of the world's largest reinsurers, writing more than $8 billion a year in net premiums. The company employs 3,500 people around the world — 750 of them in the Kansas City area.

GE ERC was founded in 1914 in Kansas City, Missouri by E.G. Trimble, an attorney and businessman. In the early days, Trimble's company, known as Employers Indemnity Corporation, sold "laundry insurance." For a penny extra, a customer could purchase insurance to cover losses if their laundry was damaged or destroyed. Over the years, Trimble's company grew to be a leader in writing workers compensation insurance and was renamed Employers Reinsurance Corporation (ERC).

A General Electric company since 1984, ERC embraces GE's core values of delivering superior service, achieving financial strength, and demonstrating an unrelenting passion for its customers. GE ERC employs the best and the brightest from around the world, because risk management is a business that requires superior analytical and technical skills.

As a GE business, GE ERC utilizes a host of proven resources, such as Six Sigma Quality. Six Sigma is a disciplined process, which enables the delivery of near-perfect products and services. For example, customers can access GE ERC's broad array of products and services from Internet sites such as *myreinsurance.com* and *cybercomp.com*. These Web sites add efficiency and speed to the business— transactions that used to take five days now take just five minutes.

GE ERC is one of the most financially secure reinsurers in the world, writing more than $8 billion a year in net premiums.

GE ERC also is one of the most financially secure reinsurers in the world, consistently earning the highest financial ratings from Standard & Poor's, A.M. Best, and Moody's.

GE ERC is committed to the community. Employees volunteer their time to causes such as United Way, Allstars Community Outreach, and the Heart of America Shakespeare Festival. What's more, GE ERC strives to help mitigate risk through its Protecting Our Promise program, in which employee volunteers retrofit daycare centers by applying safety film to windows and securing large objects that could fall in a disaster.

GE ERC's community programs exemplify the spirit of GE and ERC: people coming together and collaborating, sharing best practices, motivated by a vision of a safer, more secure world.

GE Card Services

GE Card Services, a GE Capital business, is a leader in providing credit services to retailers and consumers. Their office, located in Merriam, hosts 800 employees.

Founded in 1932 as a provider of consumer financing for GE Appliances, GE Card Services markets private-label credit cards, commercial programs, and card-related financial services to hundreds of retailers and manufacturers across North America. GE Card Services also issues and services corporate cards for commercial customers including purchasing travel and fleet vehicles cards.

GE Card Services in Merriam, markets private-label credit cards including corporate cards, travel, and fleet vehicles cards.

GE Card Services offers clients a full range of operational, financial, and analytical support along with a broad array of customized marketing solutions designed to increase sales and customer loyalty. This philosophy of partnership has helped GE Card Services grow to nearly $24 billion in total assets and serve more than 100 million cardholders.

GE Card Services has been located in Kansas City since June 1998 and believes in supporting the diverse communities where its employees live and work. Employees donate their time and talent to charitable causes focused on children, education, and economic development.

The company has built several homes in Kansas City with Habitat for Humanity, an organization dedicated to providing decent, affordable housing to those in need.

GE Transportation Systems Global Signaling (GETS Global Signaling)

They help keep trains running safely. And they've been doing it for more than a century.

GE Transportation Systems (GETS) Global Signaling is a world-class technology company, providing integrated systems solutions for the railway industry—everything from signaling to train control systems.

GETS Global Signaling in Blue Springs, provides integrated systems solutions for the railway industry.

GETS Global Signaling was formed in September 2000 when GE Harris, an innovator of train control products and railway management services, merged with Kansas City-based Harmon Industries, a leader in signaling systems and communications.

The company employs a talented, global team of more than 1,900 employees in more than 20 countries. More than 1,100 of those employees are located in Kansas City.

These employees use GE's Six Sigma Quality principles and the ISO 9001 process to develop and deliver near-perfect products and services.

"We pride ourselves on using technology to develop customer-centric solutions that keep trains moving down the rails efficiently and safely," says Chris Yessayan, services business unit leader, GETS Global Signaling. "GETS Global Signaling is working to be the pre-eminent solutions provider to the railroads as the industry looks for innovative ways to reduce costs."

GE Transportation Systems, with headquarters in Erie, Pennsylvania, jointly operates a service complex with the Burlington Northern Santa Fe Railway and KC Southern in Kansas City, Kansas.

Polsinelli Shalton & Welte

Five entrepreneurial attorneys in cramped office space on Kansas City's Country Club Plaza founded a law firm in 1972. Their concept was simple enough. They would provide superior legal work in a business law practice. Highly responsive client service would be their trademark. They would keep their entrepreneurial spirit alive by staying quick on their feet and quick with their wits. And they would strive at all times to make the practice of law enjoyable and collegial.

Nearly 30 years later, the simple wisdom of that formula translates into the operating philosophy of the highly successful law firm of Polsinelli Shalton & Welte (PSW). The attorney roster may have grown from five to more than 130. The cramped office may have expanded to four spacious locations, including the firm's main office, still on the Country Club Plaza, and offices in Overland Park, Topeka, and St. Louis. The scope of work may have developed to encompass nearly 30 practice areas. Still, Polsinelli Shalton & Welte is a business law firm. Its trademark remains superior legal work combined with outstanding client service. Entrepreneurial spirit keeps the firm striving for even greater success. As to keeping the practice of law enjoyable and collegial? Well, the firm has been successful at that as well.

The law firm of Polsinelli Shalton & Welte, P.C., is represented by, from left, James A. Polsinelli, David A. Welte, and Lonnie J. Shalton.

The firm began by representing small businesses and individuals. Throughout the 1980s, it broadened its practice and became known as one of the premiere small business and real estate law firms in the Midwest. In addition, Polsinelli Shalton & Welte was recognized as "the firm" in the area of economic development, zoning, and other issues of Public Law.

During the 1980s, the firm developed its trial department and added a significant products liability practice that is national in its client scope. While still representing mid-size companies, it also began to develop an institutional client base that led to the creation of a nonprofit law practice group and representation of large health-care and educational entities.

In the late 1990s, the firm added a financial services department, which created another avenue for growth and client development while further diversifying the firm's service mix.

The new millennium finds PSW keeping pace with the future through the creation of a Science and Technology Practice focused on Kansas City's growing biotechnology sector.

Today, the firm serves as outside general counsel to more than 2,000 closely-held corporations. It provides a

Attorneys and summer associates at Polsinelli Shalton & Welte team up on a community service project for Habitat for Humanity.

wide variety of legal services in areas including corporate finance, employee benefits and executive compensation, labor and employment, government affairs, intellectual property, tax, trusts and estates, and more. Specialty practices serve several industries including insurance, banking, health care, utilities, construction, and financial services.

The Polsinelli Shalton & Welte client list includes local, regional, and national enterprises that are familiar to many, including: the Stowers Institute for Medical Research, Key Corporate Capital, the University of Kansas Hospital Authority, the Kansas Speedway, Sprint, Nissan, Mazda, and Pfizer Pharmaceuticals.

The key to building such a large, diverse, and successful practice is the firm's seminal commitment to high quality legal work and customer service. Polsinelli Shalton & Welte attorneys strive to be more than a counselor to their clients.

W. Russell Welsh, Polsinelli Shalton & Welte's chief executive officer, describes the approach succinctly, "Our aim is to think like a business partner. This means going the extra mile to seek innovative and legally sound solutions that enable our clients to achieve business success. It is easy enough to tell a client that a transaction he is contemplating is impossible. Our goal is to move those transactions into the realm of 'possible.'"

"Furthermore," Welsh adds, "We recognize the speed at which business moves today. It is not enough to find the

Polsinelli Shalton & Welte makes maximum use of technology to deliver responsive service to clients. One of the firm's Information Technology professionals works on a server used for its new Internet/Intranet/Extranet service currently under development, PSW Interactive.

right solution. The right solution needs to be found and delivered on a timely basis. This is a vital component of our core concepts: service, speed, and know how."

Part of what allows Polsinelli Shalton & Welte attorneys to work so efficiently is technology. "Our business has become more technologically driven," said Welsh. "We continue to seek newer and better ways to use technology to serve our clients. In the next several months, we are making investments in technology that will put us at the leading edge of innovation among law firms, not just from the Midwest, but from anywhere in the country."

What about the commitment to make the practice of law enjoyable and collegial?

The firm consistently strives to build teamwork and effective staff relationships that lead to superior client service. It may be an impromptu party to celebrate the end of another successful year or a group outing to the Kansas City Zoo for employees and their families that adds to the firm's friendly atmosphere. Or it may be the annual firm softball tournament. This event puts attorneys, paralegals, and support staff together on teams to battle with their peers for the privilege of holding a traveling trophy.

Whatever makes the difference, one thing is clear— Polsinelli Shalton & Welte is a law firm with a unique, time-tested vision for success.

Polsinelli Shalton & Welte provided legal services that helped the Kansas Speedway find a home in Wyandotte County, Kansas. Like many national and local companies, the firm uses the Speedway's Hospitality Village to entertain clients.

Where It All BegBegan

Where It All Began

In 1906, Karl K. Kennedy and 14 prominent Los Angeles citizens created the first life insurance company based in Los Angeles—Occidental Life Insurance Company of California. By the end of the first year, the company produced more than $600,000 of life insurance in force. Meanwhile, in San Francisco, A. P. Giannini, the son of Italian immigrants, opened a small banking business in 1904. The bank was later to become the Bank of America. In 1928, Giannini's bank became Transamerica Corporation. In 1930, Transamerica Corporation acquired Occidental Life—a marriage that has lasted more than 70 years.

In May of 1999, Transamerica Corporation was acquired by AEGON, N.V., an international insurance organization headquartered in The Hague, The Netherlands. Thanks to this merger, Transamerica Occidental Life Insurance Company (TOLIC) is now a proud member of the AEGON Group, one of the world's leading life insurance and financial service organizations.

Jack Shalley, MD, examines a prospective policy with the underwriting department's Rebecca Zaike and Rodney Rhodes. Photo by Matt Nichols/Nichols & Co. Photography

Everything's Up-to-date in Kansas City

To reduce expenses and remain competitive, Transamerica Occidental Life moved its administrative operations to Kansas City from Los Angeles in 1994. Other locations were considered as well, but Kansas City's central location, high quality of life, and supportive local, state, and federal officials, cast the vote in favor of the Midwestern locale. The Town Pavilion in downtown Kansas City is the headquarters for this operation, which occupies eight floors in the 38-story building.

The first group to move from Los Angeles to Kansas City was Transamerica's life insurance operations team, which included new business processing, billing, collections, claims processing, systems support, and underwriting. Essentially, all the work related to administering individual life insurance policies is handled in Kansas City—from initial underwriting to final payment of the death benefit.

Within two years of the move, Transamerica relocated fixed annuities and long-term care insurance operations to the company's Kansas City office, the downtown skyscraper that features Transamerica's name in red lights. A few years later, a central regional marketing office was established.

A believer in the power of innovation, Transamerica installed a leading-edge workflow system based on image processing—the so-called "paperless" office where all the documents required to process business are committed to an optical disc and retrieved as necessary. This system allows instantaneous communication with the Los Angeles office and offices throughout the country.

Customer Service team members Michelle Adamson, Jordan Rupp, Sherita Stuart, and RuthAnn McElroy tend to policyholders' needs. Photo by Matt Nichols/Nichols & Co. Photography

Transamerica Occidental Life Today

Transamerica employees remain committed to the company's core purpose of helping its clients build, protect, and preserve their assets.

TOLIC provides a wide array of insurance and investment products designed for individuals, families, and businesses. To help clients build their assets there are many options, including fixed and variable annuities; cash-value insurance products; and investment products sold through Transamerica Financial Advisors, Inc., Transamerica's National Association of Securities Dealers-registered broker/dealer affiliate. In the areas of insurance, the various products offered can protect lifestyles through universal life and variable universal life insurance. Preserving clients' assets through individual and survivorship universal life insurance remains a prime objective in helping people nationally and in the Kansas City area.

Approximately 640 employees of Transamerica Insurance & Investment Group (TIIG), which markets products underwritten by TOLIC, and AEGON Technology Services are located in Kansas City. Based on life insurance in force, TOLIC is the third largest life insurance company in the United States.

"We have a wonderful and diverse mix of people here in Kansas City," said Mary Spence, vice president, human resources. "The strong work ethic of our employees, along with the application of advanced technology, has resulted in a highly-productive operation."

Company Values at Work

Respect, responsibility, integrity, ingenuity, and excellence are TIIG's key core values and company employees strive to live them each day. Fun is also an aspect of today's workplace. So when company officials had the opportunity to liven up the 2000 United Way fundraising campaign, they did just that.

"The television show 'Survivor' was a big hit last year, so we decided to hold a 'Survivor' contest of our own," said Frank LaRusso, senior vice president and chief underwriting officer. "By making a monetary donation to United Way, employees could purchase points toward having an executive of their choice kiss a pig."

LaRusso was the lucky "winner" and planted two kisses on a pig at TIIG's quarterly all-employee meeting.

"Our employees were really supportive of this contest, not just because they wanted to see a member of our executive team kiss livestock, but because they want to improve the lives of the people in our community," said

Senior executives Frank Rosa, Frank LaRusso, and Mary Spence are at the helm in Kansas City.

Photo by Matt Nichols/Nichols & Co. Photography

Frank Rosa, senior vice president, customer service and chief information officer.

After a successful United Way fund-raising campaign, TIIG plans to rally employees with a "Weakest Link" theme contest this year. So will the pig return to grace the stage at an employee meeting? "We're keeping that one a surprise," Rosa said.

HDR, Inc.

For more than 84 years, HDR, Inc. (HDR) has provided the full spectrum of architectural, engineering, and planning services to clients throughout the United States. Founded in 1917, the firm has more than 60 offices nationwide with projects across the nation and in 40 countries. Committed to the principles of quality design, technological innovation, and client satisfaction, HDR has dedicated itself to developing strong, long-lasting relationships from the very beginning.

BNSF Argentine Yard Project.

HDR began work in the Kansas City metropolitan area during the mid-1960s. Since then, HDR has grown by providing professional services throughout the Kansas, Missouri, Louisiana, Oklahoma, Illinois, and Texas region. The 80-member professional support staff in Kansas City includes civil, transportation, structural, and process engineers; environmental specialists; planners; management consultants; engineering technicians; CADD/graphic technicians; construction administrators; and administrative personnel.

HDR ranks among the top 50 U.S. firms by *Engineering News Record* since 1967. Service is what differentiates HDR from other local firms. Repeat business stands at 80 percent, both nationally and here in Kansas City, a clear indication of client satisfaction and confidence.

The 3,000 employee-owners of HDR are poised for even greater success in the future as the company expands in each of its core programs, including Transportation, Environmental and Resource Management, Water, Science and Technology, Healthcare and Justice.

Because each project and client is unique, HDR uses a team approach to project delivery. By listening to the clients and understanding the challenge each project offers, HDR builds project teams with the right combination of staff skills and experience. HDR incorporates this flexibility within a strong management structure. The firm's well-honed project management, production, and quality control processes allow the firm to consistently and effectively deliver quality, cost-effective projects on time and within budget, inspiring confidence among clients. This ability to meet and exceed expectations has allowed HDR to develop client relationships that have lasted many years.

"Today, clients expect HDR to anticipate their future needs and in many ways become their silent partner," said Richard R. Bell, Chairman and Chief Executive Officer, HDR, Inc. "We must be diligent in retaining our current architectural and engineering expertise and continue to grow an even broader base of diverse expertise such as scientists, planners, and other professionals to met the challenges of comprehensive integrated solutions."

Virtually every project HDR is involved in must be planned around its impact on the environment. By combining good science and good engineering, the firm has gained the respect of regulators throughout the country. That is why HDR is committed to staying in the forefront of new technology, in terms of both innovations in the architectural/engineering systems they design, and in the methods of delivering those services.

The Everglades, Florida—Everglades Environmental Restoration Project.

By providing a challenging and stimulating environment for its personnel and never losing site of its corporate principles, HDR has experienced steady growth, continually expanding the firm's range of services and technical skills and moving into new markets. The Kansas City office provides three of HDR's "new market" area services: Movable Bridge, Management Consulting, and Design-Build.

HDR's "Center of Expertise" for Movable Bridge services is located in the Kansas City office. HDR capabilities include movable bridge services for both highway and railroad structures of all types including bascule, vertical lift, and swing type bridges, as well as railroad turntables. Other areas of expertise include machinery, hydraulics, relay controls, Programmable Logic Controls (PLC), and Supervisory Control and Data Acquisition (SCADA). HDR professionals have experience with most major railroads, many State Departments of Transportation, and local municipality bridge owners across the U.S., Canada, and Mexico.

HDR Design-Build, Inc., headquartered in Kansas City, was created in April 2000 as a wholly owned subsidiary for the primary purpose of pursuing and executing design-build "at risk" projects itself or in partnership with other partners such as general construction firms, suppliers, subcontractors and/or operators. Some of the earliest projects in HDR's history were design-build, which offer a shorter project time frame, potential cost savings, and tighter integration between the designer and contractor, allowing the designers the ability to add value to construction projects. The staff includes professionals experienced in construction management, procurement, scheduling, costing, and construction administration/inspection.

HDR's Management Consulting program is focused on the provision of services to public sector clients, which improves quality and reduces costs through application of services such as bid-to-goal, managed competition and public-private partnerships, decision support systems, strategic planning, competitive business planning, training, and labor relations. Strategic areas of implementation include:

HDR Consulting, which operates within the healthcare business unit, provides strategic planning, facility planning, and clinical planning.

- Program Management — the management of public sector projects or programs from conception through completion
- Asset Management — focused on assisting clients in improving quality and reducing costs of public services by optimizing lifecycle value of public assets.
- Urban Planning — the development or improvement of the environment with the prime focus on quality of life and economic viability of communities.
- E-Government — focused on assisting clients in identifying and making provisions to embrace new technologies in order to ensure the community is well positioned to participate in and take advantage of the E-driven environment.

With HDR's talented and dedicated staff and proven formula for project success, HDR, Inc. is poised to help clients meet the challenges of the next century.

Route 367.

Bibb and Associates, Inc.

The engineering/architectural (E/A) team of Bibb and Associates, Inc., offers a full scale of services ranging from civil, structural, mechanical, and electrical engineering to architectural and interior design. Dedicated to providing the highest quality services, regardless of how large or small the project, Bibb has proven that by remaining creative in the search for excellence in engineering and architectural solutions, there is no limit to what it can achieve.

Owned by Peter Kiewit Sons', Inc., a Top 10 Construction company based in Omaha, Nebraska, Bibb's headquarters is in Lenexa, Kansas. Bibb also has a western region office in Pasadena, California.

Bibb is committed to being "the best E/A in the business." This commitment is reflected in the company's values—client service, employees, company quality, and project performance.

- Client Service: Bibb employees display a strong spirit of commitment to its clients, striving to understand their needs and working diligently to meet client expectations.

- Employees: Bibb is dedicated to developing creative, innovative professionals who provide exceptional service to every project. Employees become involved in the details of every project; they focus on getting results while never losing sight of project schedules and budgets.

Our employees hard at work, remaining committed to quality.

- Company Quality: Bibb's Company Quality Plan out lines its commitment to quality and the responsibility of every Bibb employee in assuring that it delivers the highest quality services. Bibb associates believe "Quality is the Responsibility of Every Bibb Employee."

- Project Performance: Projects are what Bibb does. At Bibb, processes define how to plan and execute work. Bibb's management structure is flat, and managers are hands-on.

Bibb's Power Division works with clients on a worldwide scale, striving to be a leader in EPC design/build power projects. The Industrial and Architecture Division provides design and project implementation services to industrial, commercial, institutional, and government clients. The Process Division, located in Pasadena, California, maintains a strong process and geothermal background.

Over the past 21 years, Bibb has created a niche in the engineering market by "getting mad and excited about company business." Employees carry a sense of personal pride for the work they do. This philosophy is the driving force behind Bibb's quest to be "the best E/A on earth."

Bibb and Associates, Inc., Corporate Headquarters,
8455 Lenexa Drive, Lenexa, Kansas 66214.

Blackwell Sanders Peper Martin

With an incredible list of business clients, Blackwell Sanders Peper Martin is one of the largest business-based law firms in the Midwest. The commercial-based law firm has more than 320 lawyers located in offices in Kansas City, Overland Park, Omaha, St. Louis, Springfield, Washington, D.C., and London. Blackwell Sanders ranks as the second largest law firm in Kansas City, according to *Ingram's Magazine* and *The Kansas City Business Journal*.

David A. Fenley, chair of Blackwell Sanders Peper Martin LLP.

Blackwell Sanders Peper Martin offers clients unparalleled strength in over 40 areas, including corporate and securities, mergers and acquisitions, labor and employment, education, real estate, tax, and commercial litigation. Areas of new innovation include intellectual property, white-collar crime, technology, and venture capital.

Locally, the firm has enjoyed a 25-year relationship with UtiliCorp United Inc. and its principle subsidiary, Aquila, Inc. UtiliCorp serves over 4 million utility customers in the U.S. and abroad and was recently ranked 147th among the Fortune Global 500 list of publicly traded companies. Aquila is a leading wholesale marketer of natural gas and electricity and an innovative provider of risk management products and services. Blackwell Sanders Peper Martin has represented UtiliCorp through national and international expansion, and the recent IPO of its subsidiary Aquila.

The firm's impressive client list continues with Hallmark Cards Incorporated, Applebee's, St. Luke's-Shawnee Mission Health System, Commerce Bancshares, Associated Wholesale Grocers, Business Men's Assurance Corporation, *The Kansas City Star*, Payless Cashways, and Highwoods Properties to name a few.

Dave Fenley, chairman and 20-plus year veteran of the firm, said the firm is proud to serve the top clients in Kansas City.

"We have a top business client list—the reason we have it is because we listen carefully to the client and work hard to understand their business needs," Fenley said.

"Our firm is committed to turning legal matters around quickly for the client, and to providing sophisticated solutions to pressing needs."

To improve and increase communications with clients, attorneys offer seminars on timely topics to business leaders, Continuing Legal Education courses to in-house counsel, and contribute to the Blackwell Sanders Web site.

Blackwell Sanders topped *Law Office Computing* magazine's list of best law office Web Sites of 2000. The Blackwell Sanders site averages 250,000 hits per month and includes links to articles written by the firm's attorneys.

The firm was founded in 1916 in Kansas City and remains committed to its roots. Blackwell Sanders employs over 800 people; of that number, more than 200 are attorneys working in the Kansas City area. Members of the firm are active in local and state politics and The Greater Kansas City Chamber of Commerce, and they have a long history of supporting the Nelson-Atkins Museum of Art.

Blackwell Sanders attorneys with client, Applebee's. Pictured from left: James M. Ash, partner with Blackwell Sanders; Robert T. Steinkamp, vice president, secretary, and general counsel with Applebee's; Shari L. Wright, of counsel with Blackwell Sanders; and George D. Shadid, executive vice president and chief financial officer with Applebee's.

Bryan Cave LLP

Bryan Cave is one of the nation's leading corporate transactional and litigation law firms with more than 600 lawyers located in 18 offices in the United States and around the world. With offices in the heart of downtown Kansas City and southern Johnson County along College Boulevard, Bryan Cave is the first choice of business clients throughout the region because of its innovation, excellence and the peace of mind that it brings.

At Bryan Cave, experienced lawyers serve as mentors. The firm's passion about our clients' businesses assures that clients receive the expertise and counsel they deserve.

Bryan Cave's watchwords of "vision in practice" are recognized by its stellar list of clients, including, among many others, H&R Block, Sprint, Ferrellgas, Bank of America, GMAC Commercial Mortgage, Blue Cross/ Blue Shield of Kansas City, Bernstein-Rein Advertising, Boeing, American Airlines, Lucent Technology, and DaimlerChrysler. Recognized nationally for its innovative application of technology, Bryan Cave has not only been a leader in incorporating electronic presentation at trials and electronic briefs filed in courts, but also has developed its own Web-enabled products and legal service. One of these, TradeZone, offers advice and a decision tree on import and export regulation questions. Developed by Bryan Cave's own lawyers and Web designers, TradeZone enables clients to quickly and cost-effectively answer questions that avoid costly pitfalls in international trade.

In NoZone, Bryan Cave has developed an online training program to enable supervisors in companies around the country to limit and even avoid liability in the area of harassment and discrimination. This Web-based program provides an up-to-date training experience, tailored to the individual business and available anywhere and at anytime. Companies across the country now have put it to use for thousands of supervisors.

"Our commitment at Bryan Cave," says Irv Belzer, resident manager of the Kansas City and Johnson County offices, "is to thoroughly learn our clients' businesses and not just to solve particular problems. We are committed to anticipating client needs and to preventative approaches. We do this through acting as one firm and calling on the extensive resources in our network to bring the best value to our clients. We take our client relationships personally."

Bryan Cave's strength derives in large part from its local roots, and its commitment to the Greater Kansas City community is well known. Bryan Cave's lawyers are involved in more than 40 not-for-profit organizations in the Greater Kansas City area and have either initiated or been called upon to handle many of the most visible issues affecting the area. Bryan Cave partners have been designated as head of the Mayor's transition team, board members on the Civic Council and Greater Kansas City, Chamber of Commerce, chaired the Charter Review Commission, and were instrumental in founding the Kansas City Trollies and in refurbishing the Folly Theater. In community efforts as in client relationships, Bryan Cave strives to anticipate, innovate, and effectively implement.

While global in geography and perspective, Bryan Cave's lawyers are committed to helping the Kansas City community and its businesses grow and prosper. Above, Bryan Cave's downtown office.

B ased on their worldwide accomplishments, Black & Veatch, Burns & McDonnell, and HNTB—three Kansas City-based, national leaders in the engineering/architectural industry—continue to set the standard for expertise, innovation, and integrity. With combined experience of more than 270 years, these firms provide state-of-the-art design of bridges, roads, airports, water treatment plants, community master plans, power plants, stadiums, and more—in Kansas City, the United States, and the rest of the world.

World Class Professionals

The expertise of these three great companies goes far beyond engineering and architecture. The technicians, urban planners, scientists, interior designers, contractors, and other professionals offer a multidisciplinary approach to delivering innovative solutions to complex problems. In addition, these vision-oriented firms offer unparalleled geographic and service diversity from more than 170 offices nationwide. Principals from each firm serve as leaders of civic and professional organizations at the local and global level. "In the same way that our geographic reach has expanded, so has the breadth, depth, and sophistication of our services to our clients, who themselves are operating in a world of accelerated change," said Black & Veatch Chairman, President, and CEO Len C. Rodman. "We embrace the responsibility of stewardship in our work as engineers, constructors, business people and citizens of the world."

Putting the Client First

"Our firms touch citizens' lives on a daily basis. We design and create the infrastructure that enhances their quality of life," states Scott Smith, HNTB senior vice president. "We listen to our clients, anticipate their needs, and deliver exemplary service and management," continues Becky Cotton Zahner, HNTB vice president.

Jeffrey Energy Center supplies approximately 33 percent of Western Resources total electric generation, and is one of the lowest generated energy cost power plants of its size and type in the United States. Black & Veatch provided development support, engineering design, procurement, and startup.

Shaping Kansas City

The presence of these three firms is highly visible and noteworthy throughout the greater Kansas City metropolitan area with projects such as: Kansas City International Airport; Major Investment Study, I-70; Kansas Speedway; NNSA's Kansas City Plant; Bruce R. Watkins Drive; Bartle Hall; Hawthorn Unit 5 Rebuild; American Royal; Kansas City Water Department; Kansas City Scout Intelligent Transportation System; and Blue Cross Blue Shield IT Infrastructure.

Global Influence

A vast array of successful, landmark projects dominate the national and international landscape: San Diego Convention Center, INVESCO Field at Mile High, Midway Airport, Everglades Restoration, Philadelphia International Airport, F-22 Robotic Coating Facility, Charles River Bridge, Jet Engine Testing Facility (Xiamen, China), National Missile Defense Program (Marshall Islands), Tenaga Nasional Berhad (Malaysia), TECO San Jose (Guatemala), and China's Yellow River Diversion. Burns & McDonnell CEO Dave Ruf explains the firms' reach and impact. "From Kansas City, all three firms have exported midwestern ingenuity around the world. I don't think it's a coincidence that these firms call Kansas City home. The work ethic, perseverance, and inventiveness of our employees prove that the well-known Kansas City Spirit is alive and well."

Left: At the Kansas Speedway, a sold-out crowd cheers the start of the inaugural NASCAR Winston Cup Series Protection One 400. HNTB led the planning, design, construction administration, and engineering/inspection team. Photo by Tom Donohue.
Right: This award winning coating facility for the U.S. Air Force's brand-new F-22 fighter is one example of the work Burns & McDonnell performs for our nation's defense.

11

Chapter Eleven

EDUCATION & QUALITY OF LIFE

The University of Health Sciences

As the academic center for Missouri's largest medical school, The University of Health Sciences College of Osteopathic Medicine plays a critical role in preparing and equipping tomorrow's physicians with the latest technology and scientific breakthroughs. Through its mission, the University is committed to educating professionals who value the human and medical needs of their patients above all other concerns.

It is with this education and philosophy that graduates of UHS become leaders in the world of medicine and as members of the community in which they live.

Leadership is the first of the University's six core values—the others are humility, faith and positivity, integrity, compassion, and service. For UHS students, the concept of healing is more than science.

Leading the way since 1995 is University President and Chief Executive Officer Karen L. Pletz, J.D. She is the first woman to fill the top spot at UHS. A Kansas City native, Pletz servers as a community leader in many capacities at the local, state, and national levels. Her leadership, through a team of excellent administrators and faculty, has positioned UHS as a leader among medical schools in the United States. Accredited by the North Central Association of Colleges and Schools as well as the American Osteopathic Association, UHS offers a four-year medical education program, followed by advanced postdoctoral training in a broad spectrum of medical specialties. The University also offers graduate medical education programs—jointly sponsored by Health Midwest's Medical Center of Independence—in surgery, internal medicine, family medicine, and orthopedics.

USH President and Chief Executive Officer Karen L. Pletz, J.D., and the Reverend Edward Kinerk, S.J., president of Rockhurst University, applaud the signing of the dual degree program agreement. (Standing, from left) Douglas C. Dalzell, J.D., UHS vice president for institutional development/corporate planning; Duane T. Brandau, D.O., Ph.D., UHS vice dean/ predoctoral and community programs; Michael Tansey, Ph.D., director of the Rockhurst Health Care Leadership Program; and Nehad I. El-Sawi, Ph.D., UHS associate dean/curriculum and education, look on.

"Just as leadership is really a relationship, quality in what we do is a direct result of motivation; the desire to do it better. Our desire to achieve quality is founded upon our values as individuals, and the degree to which our organizations' values are aligned with our personal values," said Pletz. "What we stand for as a university is what we stand for individually, and what we accomplish as a university is directly related to matching people and endeavors in a fundamental sharing of values. By so doing, we not only better the University, we better ourselves as human beings."

A Leader in the Community

Leadership in the health sciences is just one way UHS contributes to the quality of life in the Kansas City area.

As one of eight research partners in Kansas City's Life Sciences Institute, UHS has formalized a collaboration agreement with The Stowers Institute, a $200 million research facility opened in late 2000. The Stowers Institute, along with its medical research partners, is expected to draw top scientists, researchers, and physicians to the

Leadership in community service is a high priority at the University. More than 100,000 hours of community service are given by staff, faculty, and students each year.

The Educational Pavilion, opened in 1996.

Kansas City area, creating a national center for biomedical research. The Stowers-UHS collaboration encompasses academic appointments, program development, and integrated graduate programs, as well as scientific and technical resources for public and private research sponsors.

To further its commitment to Kansas City's Life Sciences endeavor and as a component of its mission, UHS has raised private funds as part of Campaign 2000, a capital drive to construct a 65,000-square-foot Life Sciences Research and Education Center. The new center breaks ground in January 2002 and will house research laboratories and clinical conference rooms.

The completion of this building will increase the University's ability to expand translational research activity currently being conducted on campus. University researchers are funded by the National Institutes of Health, focusing in the areas of cancer prevention and cure.

The new building will also house Score One for Health— a healthscreening program for elementary school students in the city's urban core. The UHS program, partially funded by the Kauffman Foundation, is a cooperative effort with the Kansas City Missouri Public School District as well as Raytown and Grandview School Districts. As an additional commitment to the inner city, UHS partners to provide access to technology for at-risk persons in the Northeast area of the city, as well as not-for-profit agencies, including the Don Bosco Center, Della C. Lamb Community Center, Newhouse, and Boys and Girls Clubs. UHS offers technical support, troubleshooting, and training opportunities for these agencies as a vital link in the Community Service Network.

In another innovative leadership endeavor, the University partners with Rockhurst University to offer medical students enrolled in the Doctor of Osteopathic Medicine (D.O.) degree program, the opportunity to earn an MBA while preparing to become a physician. UHS is one of only two U.S. universities to offer a fully integrated dual-degree program. Developed especially for UHS students, the Rockhurst MBA in Health Care Leadership complements UHS students' medical education by helping develop physician-managers of competence and conscience with the business and leadership skills necessary to manage costs while providing quality holistic care. The new program's mission is to produce caring, compassionate physicians with the knowledge to navigate today's health-care system.

"Future physicians will become conversant in the language of business and how business practices and processes work together to create efficient managerial systems.

"We believe that by providing our medical students with additional education in the business aspects of health care, they will enhance their service to their patients and their contributions to the quality of health care in the United States," Pletz said.

UHS students spend many hours each year in the local grade schools performing basic physicals of school children.

The Administration Building, built in 1916 and recently totally renovated.

Beginning the first week of orientation, UHS emphasizes values and getting involved. Each entering student participates in a day of community service, emphasizing the values that are the components in the University's mission: leadership, humility, faith and positivity, integrity, compassion, and service. Throughout the students' four years of medical education these values are a focus. UHS students, faculty, and staff contribute more than 100,000 hours of community service each year.

A Commitment to Academic Excellence

Since 1916 UHS has graduated nearly 6,500 physicians. Today, 5,000 UHS alumni practice medicine across the country in a variety of specialty fields, many in underserved areas. A UHS education prepares students for residency training in any area of medical specialty, including surgery, anesthesiology, psychiatry, gynecology, obstetrics, cardiology, pediatrics, neurology, ophthalmology, oncology, and additional subspecialties. UHS students'

University lab session.

Kemmy M. Mizinga, Ph.D., associate professor of pharmacology, is integral to many of the research efforts at The University of Health Sciences.

Ricci Auditorium seats approximately 260 students and is primarily used as the academic learning center for first year curriculum.

performance on National Board Licensing Examinations is consistently high. In 1997, UHS became one of the first medical schools in the country to require passage of the National Medical Boards in order to graduate.

Average enrollment is approximately 850 students. Nearly 4,000 students apply for 225 first year seats every year. Students range in age and come from a wide variety of cultural backgrounds.

During their first two years at UHS, students participate in an award-winning curriculum, newly designed to achieve earlier integration of the clinical and basic sciences. In a clinical presentation-based track, students learn the human application of every aspect of medicine including anatomy, biochemistry, histology, physiology, microbiology, pathology, and pharmacology.

In their third and fourth years, students receive advanced clinical training from rural clinics to prestigious urban hospitals across the country, including 30 hospitals in the Kansas City metropolitan area. UHS has a formal clinical education affiliation with Health Midwest in which students in Kansas City do their clinical rotations throughout the Health Midwest hospital and clinic system.

A nationally recognized leader in medical education, UHS is the first osteopathic medical school in the country to win the John Templeton Foundation Spirituality in Medicine Award, alongside eight leading U.S. medical schools, including Harvard University.

Founded in 1916, the University of Health Sciences is located on a 10-acre campus in the northeast sector of downtown Kansas City. Since 1995, the University has expanded with two new buildings. Dedicated in 1996, the Educational Pavilion is an innovative learning center designed for the future. This $10 million, 96,000-square-foot facility features high-tech amenities such as a spacious auditorium with a sophisticated audio-visual system. The Pavilion incorporates labs specially designed to facilitate

learning, as well as faculty offices, meeting rooms, a cafeteria, and a well-equipped sports medicine center. In June 2000, the Mary L. Butterworth, D.O., Alumni Center opened as a center for community and alumuni activities. It also houses the University office of advancement.

With 9 applicants for each seat in the first-year class, acceptance at UHS is highly competitive. Ready to greet eager medical students is a faculty that is unmatched in quality, spirit, and knowledge. In addition, more than 300 community clinical UHS faculty members are practicing physicians, so they offer students real insight to the world of medicine.

The University of Health Sciences is a shining example of leadership in Kansas City, in academic excellence, partnerships in education, and community service. ▩

President and Chief Executive Officer Karen L. Pletz, J.D., welcomes new students to the reception following the White Coating Ceremony, a program designed to emphasize to students the importance of compassion in medicine.

Rockhurst University

Rockhurst University was founded in 1910 with a vision inspired by the teachings of St. Ignatius Loyola that focused on educating the whole person. Today, Rockhurst University devotes its core curriculum to personal and professional growth, and developing students into leaders with competence, compassion, and conscience.

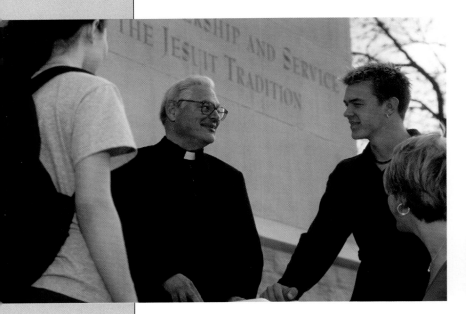

Rockhurst University is committed to learning, leadership, and service in the Jesuit tradition.

Rockhurst University is one of 28 Jesuit universities and colleges in the United States. It is ranked among the top 15 Midwest master's universities by *U.S. News & World Report*, as well as one of the "Best Buys" in the Midwest. Peterson's Competitive Colleges has Rockhurst University ranked among the top 10 percent of all colleges and universities in the country.

The university welcomes students and faculty from various religious backgrounds and value systems. About 3,000 Christian and non-Christian students, as well as those from ethical and humanitarian traditions not based in religion, come from 26 states and 20 foreign countries to attend classes at Rockhurst University.

Rockhurst offers 31 undergraduate programs and six graduate programs, including the largest MBA program in the Kansas City metropolitan area. Rockhurst is also renowned for its Executive Fellows MBA program for mid- and upper-level managers. Master's programs are also offered in communication sciences and disorders, occupational and physical therapy, and education.

Leaders throughout the Kansas City area are invited to participate in the university's Center for Leadership. The center serves to spark the imagination and social inventiveness and support the development of these

leaders. It also seeks to provide the necessary tools and resources to help our leaders better meet the challenges they will face, both today and in the future.

The campus of Rockhurst University reaches prominently across 55 acres located in Kansas City's cultural, research, and educational district, just south of the Country Club Plaza. At the heart of the campus is the Bell Tower, a structure that bares the inscription, "Learning, leadership, and service in the Jesuit tradition." These words summarize the mission of Rockhurst University and capture the spirit in which the university carries out its work.

The primary emphasis of the university is instructional excellence. The university offers a professionally qualified faculty that is student-oriented, and 86 percent of the faculty hold a terminal degree in their field. A student/faculty ratio of 12:1 provides for a close student-faculty relationship and gives students opportunities to develop their own leadership skills through group projects, oral presentations, and classroom discussion.

Bells ring every hour from Rockhurst's 85-foot bell tower, the most striking and visible landmark of the campus.

In keeping with the school's mission of promoting compassion and conscience, many students voluntarily participate in service-related projects. Approximately 85 percent of undergraduates take part in service projects throughout the Kansas City metropolitan area. University-sponsored trips to areas such as Central America, South America, and Mexico allow students to serve others who are less fortunate. Each year Rockhurst University students donate more than 25,000 hours of their own time to others in need.

Students at Rockhurst University also gain first-hand experience in their chosen fields through a variety of avenues ranging from professional internships to research projects. Students gain valuable "real-world" experience through internship programs with companies such as Hallmark Cards, Sprint, Starlight Theatre, Intertec Publishing, IBM, and the Kansas City Chiefs.

Rockhurst University established the Thomas More Center for the Study of Catholic Thought and Culture in the spring of 2000. The center, named after the university's

Whether in the classroom, through an internship, or as part of an organization, Rockhurst students are making a difference in Kansas City and beyond.

patron saint, promotes critical and committed analysis of the Catholic tradition. Its thought-provoking programs solicit discussion of all aspects of Catholicism, including literature, history, fine arts, philosophy, theology, and the social sciences.

Among the recent additions to the campus are the Greenlease Gallery and a student social activities hall. The gallery holds the university's collection of religious art, as well as changing displays of works by local and national artists. It is also the site of readings for the Midwest Poet Series and other literary readings and receptions. Future plans include expansion of the soccer field and creation of Loyola Park, a complex consisting of a new baseball stadium, tennis courts, and a jogging path.

The university is a member of the National Collegiate Athletic Association, with its many athletic programs competing at the NCAA Division II level. A member of the Heartland Conference, Rockhurst University fields 10 varsity sports that include men's and women's basketball, golf, soccer, and tennis, as well as baseball and women's volleyball. The university's soccer, volleyball, and baseball teams have all been ranked nationally. Rugby, cross-country, and lacrosse are offered as club sports and students may also participate in a vast intramural program that includes 30 different sports and events.

Rockhurst University has been guided since June 1998 by the Reverend Edward Kinerk, S.J., the first alumnus of Rockhurst to serve as its president.

Rockhurst is ranked among the top 15 Midwest master's universities by U.S. News & World Report.

K ansas City might once have been a rough frontier town somewhere between places synonymous with arts and culture, but today it is at the heart of it all—setting a pace nationwide with its growth in arts opportunities for every citizen. A vigorous cultural diversity infuses every part of the metro region. It guarantees arts experiences reflecting the heritage of entire peoples, as well as those expressing unique points of view. It gives Kansas City an extraordinary texture and vitality—promising the region's people a very special quality of life.

Any day or night Kansas City makes art a part of real life with celebrations, performances, public art, exhibits, galleries, lessons, museums, and private collections often visible in public places. More than 300 arts and cultural organizations make this possible, and The Arts Council of Metropolitan Kansas City serves as a collective voice for all of them, helping represent the interests of the arts community in the civic arena.

The Arts Council is the umbrella arts advocacy organization for the Kansas City region. It assures that public dialogue includes accurate information about what arts and culture mean to shared community goals in the five-county, two-state metropolitan area.

The Arts Council also creates system-wide services and programs to help organizations with activities that may be more effective if shared. It works in the community to understand ways that arts and culture can support a better quality of life for everyone—and be supported in return.

In metropolitan Kansas City there was no overall organization of the arts across geographic boundaries until March 1999, when private funding was generated through the Greater Kansas City Community Foundation (GKCCF) and the Muriel McBrien Kauffman Foundation to create an organization with enough capacity and reach to make a difference in the arts for organizations and individuals region-wide. Additional funding was provided by the Wallace-Reader's Digest Fund and the Missouri Arts Council, a state agency.

With the Arts Council of Metropolitan Kansas City as a convening organization, the arts community is developing a "critical mass" of shared energy for arts and culture in an increasingly busy, diverse, ambitious, challenged, and hopeful arts environment. The leadership and staff of arts and cultural organizations throughout the metroplex have made the Arts Council a forum for ideas and action.

The Arts Council's vision includes increasing services that will:

- connect individuals, families, and neighborhoods to arts and cultural activities that meet their wants and needs. This includes helping the community find ways to support arts organizations that assure experiences and participation in the arts to all people;
- promote business and arts and cultural partnerships that benefit businesses, their employees, and the economic development of our community;

The Kansas City Symphony

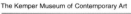
The Kemper Museum of Contemporary Art

The Theater in the Park

Anthony Krutzkamp of the Kansas City Ballet. Photographer: Ken Coit

Kansas City
Friends of
Alvin Ailley

The Lyric Opera of Kansas City

"Always" by Clement Meadmore
Courtesy of Johnson County Community College

Photo by Mark MacDonald, courtesy of
Kansas City Starlight Theatre

- increase the connection of young people to the arts through arts and cultural experiences both in and out of school;
- recognize and promote community and neighborhood arts and cultural programs throughout metropolitan Kansas City.

The Arts Council has successfully launched region-serving programs, including:

- **Kansas City Business Committee for the Arts**, to promote understanding that arts and culture not only enrich our lives but also contribute to the economic vitality of the area. More and more companies are recognizing that business needs arts and culture to attract and keep employees and increase the quality of working life. Launched by the Arts Council of Metropolitan Kansas City in 2001, the Kansas City Business Committee for the Arts is an affiliate of the national Business Committee for the Arts, Inc., founded by David Rockefeller in 1967 to develop strategic alliances between business and the arts;
- **Studio 150**™, a job-training program in the arts for area youth. Young people 15 to 19 from the five-county area work with professional artists in a summer work program in painting, sculpture, ceramics, and dance;
- **Workshops and Roundtables**, education and net working opportunities on topics ranging from fundraising to strategic planning to cultural tourism.

The Arts Council provides arts organizations and the community they serve a common ground to address shared goals. The Arts Council of Metropolitan Kansas City is located in offices in the Crossroads Arts District at 1925 Central, Suite 150, Kansas City, Missouri, providing a centralized and readily accessible meeting place for arts organizations.

The Arts Council offers ArtsLinks, the on-line home for arts and culture in the area: www.ArtsLinks.org. This user-friendly interactive cultural calendar and database provides easy access around-the-clock to information about arts events, organizations, and opportunities in the five-county area. It also links to www.artistsregister. com/missouri, which showcases the visual artists of Missouri and Metropolitan Kansas City. Joan Israelite, Chief Executive Officer of the Arts Council, can be reached at 816-221-1777 and at israel@artslinks.org.

Johnson County Community College

As the world moves further into the Information Age, the importance of lifelong learning will become even more crucial as people re-skill themselves to stay current and achieve their goals. That's why learning comes first at Johnson County Community College, a two-year comprehensive community college that continues to grow as it meets the needs of the developing community.

Founded in 1969, JCCC is Kansas' third largest institution of higher education and the largest of its 19 community colleges. More than 17,000 credit students and about 18,000 continuing education students attend classes each semester. Students range in age from 18 to 80.

earn a bachelor's degree from a four-year school through one of JCCC's many partnerships with Kansas and Missouri colleges and universities.

The community college offers the most comprehensive continuing education program in the Kansas City area. The Center for Business and Technology plays a key role in providing workforce development in management and supervisory skills, as well as the latest training available in computer software and information technology. Since 1983, the Center for Business and Technology has served more than 153,000 employees from more than 2,500 businesses. JCCC also assists local companies in applying for grants available from the Kansas Department of Commerce. Small business owners can receive free management consulting and technical assistance from the Small Business Development Center housed on campus. In addition, more than 12,000 people each year take advantage of the school's more than 600 certification, recertification, and relicensure courses of study offered by the Center for Professional Education. And more than 9,000 people a year learn how to enjoy their leisure time by attending one of JCCC's personal enrichment courses.

JCCC returns about $3.95 to the community for every tax dollar it collects. Its net economic impact on the community is more than $290 million annually.

Students find everything they need—from academic advising through registration to financial aid—under one roof in JCCC's Student Center.

JCCC provides a strong transfer program, a viable career program, and a high-quality continuing-education program designed to meet learners' need for personal and professional development. The college offers associate of arts, associate of science and associate of applied science degrees as well as career program certificates. A full range of undergraduate credit courses form the first two years of most college curricula. The college has more than 100 transfer agreements with regional colleges and universities, which assure admittance without loss of time or credit. In addition, more than 50 one- and two-year career degree and certificate programs prepare students to enter the job market in high-employment fields. It's even possible for students to attend classes on the JCCC campus and

Students take a break from classes in the Commons Courtyard on the JCCC campus.

La Petite Academy, Inc.

Whether it is heading to the office or out of town for a business trip, parents trust their children to the care and expertise of the professionals of La Petite Academy.

La Petite Academy, Inc., is the nation's largest privately held early childhood education company with more than 700 schools in 36 states and the District of Columbia. With headquarters in Overland Park, Kansas, La Petite Academy, Inc., provides developmental opportunities for approximately 87,000 children from infant to early childhood education and after school programs. Twenty-eight La Petite Academies dot the Kansas City area.

La Petite Academies deliver the La Petite Journey® curriculum, a preschool curriculum based on the early learning goals outlined by the National Association for the Education of Young Children (NAEYC). The La Petite Journey combines a mix of hands-on, developmentally and age-appropriate activities for preschoolers. Lesson plans are devised to incorporate the alphabet, numbers, reading, art, music, and playtime. The program includes a blend of self-directed student activities as well as teacher instruction. All aspects of total learning are addressed— physical, emotional, social, language, and cognitive.

An innovative new service for parents who travel began February 2001, with the launch of La Petite Academy's new Kids Station Passport℠ Program. The program, geared to children ages six weeks to 12 years old, gives parents access to short-term child services at any

La Petite Academy in the country, located near the parents' business, vacation, or conference destination.

The program provides high-quality early childhood education and skilled care for children in a safe, friendly environment, enabling parents to take their children with them on business or pleasure trips. Passport is available to current La Petite families and to those who are not currently enrolled at La Petite.

In July 2001, La Petite introduced a new initiative in its classrooms to teach children about the environment. To launch the project, La Petite's executive and management team built an interactive nature trail for young children in the Wetlands Park in Las Vegas. Each region of Academies has selected its own ongoing activity that reinforces environmental activism and education.

This past spring, children in all the La Petite Academies followed the journey of the first blind mountaineer to participate in the Mt. Everest climb, Erik Weihenmayer, and his trek to the top of Mt. Everest. During the three-month climb, the children communicated via e-mail with Michael O'Donnell, who was Weihenmayer's guide for the Everest 2001 climb. It was considered one of the world's largest outdoor classrooms!

In Kansas City, La Petite was a proud sponsor of Looking at Caldecott: Distinguished American Picture Books. This special exhibition at The Writers Place displayed children's books awarded the prestigious Caldecott Medal. The medal, given since 1938 to the illustrator of the most distinguished American picture book for children by the Association of Library Service to Children, helps instill a love for reading in children.

Under the La Petite Academy umbrella, the Montessori Unlimited preschool represents the largest (32), most consistent chain of schools offering the Montessori approach to learning. In 1998, the company announced an investment by J. P. Morgan Partners (JPMP), formerly Chase Capital Partners, and a global partnership with more than $24 million under management. J. P. Morgan Partners' primary limited partner is J. P. Morgan Chase & Co., one of the largest financial institutions in the United States. ▩

Above: A crowd gathers as a La Petite teacher reads to the group.
Right: A La Petite Director says goodbye to a student after talking with the family.

The University of Kansas

Fans who attend sporting events at the University of Kansas (KU) campus in Lawrence are greeted with what Sports Illustrated Magazine calls the best yell in college sports—the Rock Chalk Chant.

But far more than Big 12 Conference action and one of the winningest basketball programs in the nation entices visitors to this large 1,000-acre campus with the small-town feel, just west of Kansas City.

An aerial view of the KU Lawrence campus. **National Geographic** *magazine has called the Lawrence campus one of the nation's most beautiful.* Photo by David McKinney/KU

The University of Kansas, which opened in 1866, is nationally known for its academic quality. Twenty of its academic programs rank among the top 30 nationally. KU is one of the only 34 public universities granted membership in the prestigious American Association of Universities. The university is a regular on the list of the top 10 public universities for the number of National Merit scholars enrolled, and nearly 25 KU students have won Rhodes scholarships.

More than 28,000 students study in 325 degree programs at KU, which includes campuses not only in Lawrence but also in Overland Park, and medical center campuses in Kansas City and Wichita.

Learning and research opportunities for students are enhanced by KU's role as a major research university with annual research funding near $200 million. The research enterprise allows for collaborations with businesses and, most important, projects that help improve the quality of life.

In Kansas City alone, KU has played an integral part in establishing the city as a major hub in two diverse areas: life sciences and telecommunications research. The Medical Center's Hoglund Brain Imaging Center, slated to open in 2003, will be one of only three facilities nationwide with the capability of safely scanning the brain of a fetus in utero.

KU has also taken a leadership position in the "next generation" Internet, commonly known as Internet2, through involvement in the Great Plains Network and the University Corporation for Advanced Internet Development (UCAID). A non-profit consortium, UCAID aims to develop a second Internet for research and education applications such as video graphics, telemedicine, digital libraries, real-time collaboration, and distance learning.

The university brings rich cultural offerings to the area. KU's museums of natural history and art are magnets to children and adults from throughout the Kansas City metropolitan area. With more than 17,000 works of art, the Spencer art museum has long been regarded as one of the top teaching museums in the nation. Speakers, artists, and musicians appear at the campus's beautiful Lied Center, a 2,000-seat state-of-the-art performing arts hall. Nearby is the 250-seat Bales Organ Recital Hall, with its cathedral-like acoustics.

With more than 60,000 KU alumni living in the Greater Kansas City area, it won't be hard to spy KU's mascot on cars, caps, and T-shirts everywhere. It's the Jayhawk, a colorful, mythical bird that dates back to pre-Civil War times.

Paola Sanguinetti (left), KU assistant professor of architecture and urban design, helps a student with a design studio class project. Photo by Doug Koch/KU University Relations

Since its inception, the University of Missouri-Kansas City (UMKC) has continually reinvented itself. Nestled on 93 acres in the heart of Kansas City, UMKC is the metropolitan area's only four-year research university, offering undergraduate, graduate, and doctoral degrees.

Chartered in 1929, the University of Kansas City began classes in the fall of 1933 on a 40-acre land grant from city patriarch William Volker. The transition from a small, liberal arts university to a public, comprehensive, four-year university called for 30 years of adaptations. The university grew primarily by acquisition and innovation, incorporating a vast array of pre-existing schools including medicine, dentistry, and law, plus new ideas in theatre, education, biological sciences, and computer science.

The University of Kansas City joined the University of Missouri System in 1963 and became the University of Missouri-Kansas City. By the end of the century, enrollment neared 13,000. UMKC accepts about 60 percent of applicants, then works diligently to ensure success through mentoring, small classes, and positive interaction between teachers and students.

Today, UMKC offers 120 undergraduate and graduate degree programs. The University's vision is to be a community of learners making the world a better place and defining the new standards for higher education.

Volker Campus. The University of Missouri-Kansas City offers 120 undergraduate, graduate, and professional degree programs and supports Kansas City through numerous university-city programs.

Throughout its evolution, UMKC's entrepreneurial spirit has led to the development of many cutting-edge programs. It created one of the first interdisciplinary Ph.D. programs in the country and the School of Interdisciplinary Computing and Engineering. The University continues to emerge as a power in life sciences research, especially in genomics, proteomics, and other emphases at the molecular level.

UMKC prides itself on a dynamic relationship with Kansas City and surrounding communities. In addition to monitoring student internships and practica in local schools, businesses, and hospitals, individual departments work directly with communities through volunteer programs, centers, and institutes to meet the needs of both students and communities. In 2000, UMKC launched the Center for the City. The center serves as a clearinghouse between the university and the city, linking faculty, staff, and students from UMKC with individuals and corporations to address economic, social, and cultural needs. The center also functions as a catalyst in building university-city partnerships.

UMKC has found its true essence in a creative profile that responds quickly to the changing needs of its students, the people of Kansas City, and its surrounding area. The University of Missouri-Kansas City is an educational institution that blends small-college environment, interaction with the academic breadth, and scope of a large research university. As well, it fosters cultural awareness and compassionate understanding in its students, to the benefit of all in the Kansas City area. 🔲

Scofield Hall, home to UMKC's College of Arts and Sciences. Academic depth and small student-faculty ratios are hallmarks of the university.

12

Chapter Twelve

HEALTH CARE & PHARMACEUTICALS

Saint Luke's-Shawnee Mission Health System

S aint Luke's-Shawnee Mission Health System's tradition of care in Kansas City began more than a century ago, when All Saints Hospital, a 50-bed facility, opened in 1882. Today, Saint Luke's-Shawnee Mission Health System (SLSMHS) is nationally recognized for its clinical outcomes. With more than 40 locations and 7,000 employees, SLSMHS treats more than 50,000 inpatients and 500,000 outpatients each year.

But despite its size, SLSMHS is known for the individualized care it provides for each patient. Customers consistently rank Saint Luke's Hospital of Kansas City and Shawnee Mission Medical Center numbers one and two among hospitals in the metropolitan area for their quality of care. And that care quality has earned several notable validations, including the Missouri Quality Award, the Kansas Award for Excellence, and the National Quality Health Care Award.

SLSMHS, formed in 1996, is committed to enhancing the physical, mental, and spiritual health of the communities it serves. SLSMHS comprises eight hospitals and a number of physician and health provider offices that provide a range of primary, acute, tertiary, and chronic care services at multiple locations throughout the Kansas City area.

For more than 100 years, Crittenton has been caring for the emotional health of children and families in the Kansas City area. It has evolved into a comprehensive system of care that includes acute inpatient hospitalization, partial hospitalization, residential treatment, outpatient treatment, community-based services, and prevention services.

Convenient Locations Throughout Kansas City

One of the hospitals of SLSMHS is Saint Luke's Hospital of Kansas City, a 650-bed tertiary care hospital offering many specialized programs and services. The Mid America Heart Institute of Saint Luke's Hospital is the region's premier cardiac center and the city's only heart transplant provider. The Heart Institute is world-renowned for its work in the diagnosis and treatment of heart diseases. Other Saint Luke's Hospital strengths include the Level I Trauma Center and Level III Neonatal Intensive Care Unit, the highest designations in the state. Saint Luke's received the Missouri Quality Award from the Excellence in Missouri Foundation in both 1995 and 1999, the only hospital to win the award twice.

More people are admitted to Saint Luke's Hospital than to any other hospital in the Kansas City area.

Shawnee Mission Medical Center is a 383-bed acute care facility that offers comprehensive medical and surgical services, 24-hour emergency services, oncology, pediatrics, urology, orthopedics, gastroenterology, ophthalmology, neurology, pulmonary medicine, cardiology, and behavioral health. It features the metro area's busiest birthing center, with more than 3,200 infants delivered annually. SMMC is also home to the nationally recognized Center for Women's Health. In 1998, SMMC received the Kansas Award for Excellence, the highest quality award in the state.

Saint Luke's Northland Hospital has two campuses—the 55-bed Barry Road Campus facility, located in Platte County, which offers acute inpatient medical and surgical services and a Level II special care nursery, and the 92-bed Smithville Campus, which provides behavioral health services, a fitness center, skilled nursing care, and inpatient rehabilitation services.

Founded in 1972, the Lee Ann Britain Infant Development Center at Shawnee Mission Medical Center serves children from across the metropolitan area who are challenged with cerebral palsy, muscular dystrophy, spina bifida, autism, Down syndrome, and many other developmental disabilities.

The hospitalist program consists of hospital-based physicians who care for hospitalized patients of referring primary care physicians. The hospitalist orders medication, rehabilitation, and follow-up care while in constant communication with the referring physician, establishing a continuity of care for hospitalized patients.

The newest SLSMHS facility is Saint Luke's South in Overland Park, Kansas. Saint Luke's South, which opened in December 1998, is a 75-bed facility with 24-hour emergency services, a 20-bed inpatient rehabilitation unit, a maternity center, and a medical office building.

Crittenton delivers comprehensive inpatient care for children and adolescents and has a network of outpatient clinics that provide assessment and treatment for adults, children, adolescents, and families.

The other two hospitals that make up SLSMHS are Wright Memorial Hospital, in Trenton, Missouri, a 53-bed community hospital with specialty outreach clinics; and Anderson County Hospital, in Garnett, Kansas, a 66-bed community hospital that provides medical and surgical services. Cabot Westside Clinic provides bilingual primary health and educational services to residents of the Westside and the Greater Kansas City area.

SLSMHS values diversity as an important aspect of quality patient care and an inclusive workplace environment. Ensuring that every patient and employee feels welcomed, respected, and appreciated is a top priority at SLSMHS. With a commitment like that, it's no wonder Kansas Citians rate Saint Luke's Hospital and Shawnee Mission Medical Center the most preferred hospitals for heart, cancer, obstetrics, emergency, and surgical services.

Spirit of Innovation

Saint-Luke's-Shawnee Mission Health System is recognized as a pioneer of new procedures and innovative clinical programs. In a recent study, SLSMHS ranks

number one in consumer preference for specialty services by area residents.

Leading the way is the Mid America Heart Institute, which continues to outperform the market in key measures of quality and is the most preferred center for heart care in Kansas City. The facility is staffed by an internationally recognized medical team that includes specialists in the areas of balloon angioplasty, open-heart surgery, cardiac electrophysiology, and cardiac imaging. The Heart Institute is the region's only heart transplant program.

Each year more than 10,000 patients with cardiovascular disease seek treatment at the Heart Institute, with 50 percent of those patients traveling to Kansas City for treatment. The Heart Institute was the first facility worldwide to apply balloon angioplasties as a way to stop heart attacks in progress. For this procedure and other cardiac emergencies, the institute is available with surgical and medical staff 24 hours a day, 7 days a week. In the way of technology, the Heart Institute is the only facility to have two dedicated cardiovascular laboratories for pacemaker implants and for electrophysiology studies, which map the electrical activity of the heart.

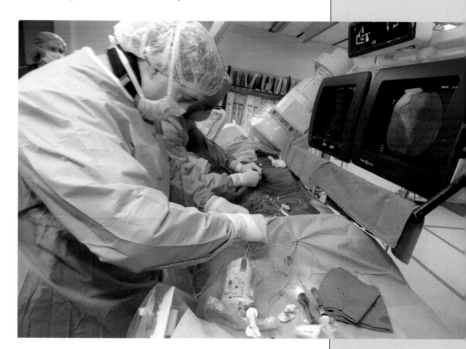

In addition to providing quality medical care, Saint Luke's Hospital and its Mid America Heart Institute are committed to education and research. The hospital is an active center of medical education and a primary teaching hospital for the University of Missouri-Kansas City School of Medicine. Saint Luke's Hospital has primary research strengths in cardiovascular research, oncology, and immunology and infectious diseases. Well over 100 new research protocols are conducted annually.

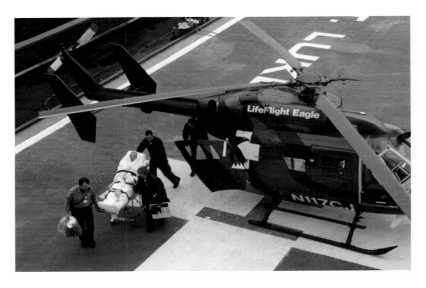

Thanks to Life Flight Eagle, patients are only minutes away from the top-notch critical care services available at Saint Luke's-Shawnee Mission Health System.

Saint Luke's Hospital is an active center of medical education and a primary teaching hospital for the University of Missouri-Kansas City School of Medicine. Saint Luke's Hospital has primary research strengths in cardiovascular research, oncology, and immunology and infectious diseases, particularly as they relate to translational research and clinical trials.

Well over 100 new research protocols are conducted annually generating more than $5 million a year in clinical trials funding. Saint Luke's Hospital is a founding member of the Alliance Research Consortium, an organization of independent medical centers dedicated to enhancing institutional participation of its members in clinical research.

Saint Luke's-Shawnee Mission Health System and Health Midwest are working to develop and create a Comprehensive Cancer Center. There is no single comprehensive cancer program for patients and their families anywhere in the five-state region. The Comprehensive Cancer Center designation is made available through the National Cancer Institute which is known for its commitment to clinical care, cancer research, professional collaboration, and community outreach.

In a joint statement, G. Richard Hastings, president and chief executive officer of SLSMHS, and Richard W. Brown, president and chief executive officer of Health Midwest, said, "Working together, we want to build upon our individual strengths in a way that will enhance the delivery of cancer services to the community. Our plan is to develop a first-class cancer center in the Midwest on par with other comprehensive cancer centers, such as the ones in Houston and Boston."

Other breakthroughs being used at SLSMHS include a new technology called mammotome, the latest in breast biopsies. Radiologists at Shawnee Mission Medical Center are using this handheld device to remove benign breast masses through a vacuum suctioned needle.

Saint Luke's Hospital and Oncology & Hematology Associates of Kansas City were the first to conduct a haploidentical stem cell transplant in the city. This procedure uses stem cells from a parent or child who is automatically half matched with the patient.

The Stroke Center at Saint Luke's Hospital received top honors for its outstanding achievements in high-quality outcomes and efficient management of stroke care. The Stroke Center was the only hospital in the region to participate in a new clot-busting therapy delivery directed to the clot in the brain artery.

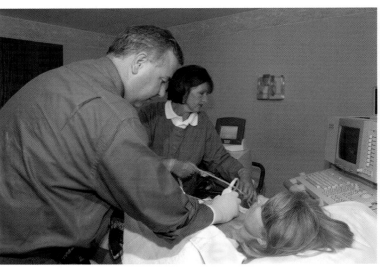

Saint Luke's-Shawnee Mission Health System's cancer services use the latest surgical, chemotherapy, and radiation therapy techniques as well as the latest diagnostic imaging and laboratory equipment to diagnose and treat cancer patients. SLSMHS provides the region's largest blood and marrow transplant program and gynecology program and has the most modern radiation therapy equipment in Kansas City.

SLSMHS has received several prestigious honors for its innovations in using on-line technology in health care. By coordinating clinical information in real time, the health system is reducing the amount of time patients stay in the hospital, improving care quality, and decreasing the transfer of patients to tertiary care facilities.

SLSMHS continues to be recognized for its quality—both for the care it provides and for its efforts to promote healthy living. Teams across SLSMHS have received prestigious awards for their efforts.

Community Outreach

Whether it is creating new service programs like the Mobile Mammography Program or the Heart Safe Community Partnership Campaign, Saint Luke's-Shawnee Mission Health System efforts are saving lives.

The Breast Care Mobile Mammography Program provides mammograms to female employees of corporations in the Kansas City area, as well as uninsured or underinsured women who lack access to screenings.

The Heart Safe Community Partnership, launched by the Mid America Heart Institute, is working to raise community awareness about the seriousness of sudden cardiac arrest, along with the vital use and role of automatic external defibrillators within the community setting at businesses, organizations, churches, and other locations.

Saint Luke's-Shawnee Mission Health System delivers nearly 7,500 babies every year—including more than 100 sets of twins. A father greets one of his newborn twin daughters with a kiss at Saint Luke's Northland Hospital-Barry Road Campus.

SLSMHS hosts and provides support for many ongoing community activities, such as the annual Kansas City Corporate Challenge. The Corporate Challenge, which has grown from 18 companies in 1980 to 145 in 2000, promotes fitness and wellness within the Kansas City business community.

SLSMHS provides support for Kansas City in numerous other ways, including providing health information and expertise for community agency boards; regional outreach programs; subsidized health services, screenings, and immunizations; support groups; clinical research; charitable grants and sponsorships; and donations of equipment and supplies.

The ASK-A-NURSE program has received overwhelming responses since its inception. Kansas Citians can call (816) 932-6220 or (800) 932-6220, 24 hours a day and obtain medical advice and health information provided by registered nurses. The service is free. ASK-A-NURSE also offers a physician referral service, has information on Saint Luke's-Shawnee Mission facilities and programs, and provides registration services for community education classes and programs.

The Saint Luke's South Inpatient Rehabilitation Unit has 20 beds and an adjacent therapy gym. It's the ideal care setting for patients who have experienced a disabling injury or illness and who are medically stable but not yet functioning at their highest possible level.

CyDex, Inc.

Since its creation in 1993, CyDex, Inc. has experienced record growth as one of the area's fastest developing pharmaceutical and biotechnology firms. An innovator in the emerging field of drug delivery technologies, CyDex continues to pave the way for advances in treatment of serious diseases.

CyDex meets an important need in the $300 billion market for pharmaceuticals and biotechnology—providing advanced formulations and delivery technologies to enable new drugs to succeed, or to improve the effectiveness or safety of existing drugs.

Promising drugs are often stopped in development because issues with the active ingredients prevent them from being absorbed in the human body, so CyDex technology can be a key to product success.

The Overland Park-based company is working with an all-star list of global pharmaceutical and biotech companies to aid in the development or improvement of drugs for diseases ranging from schizophrenia to cancer, the peak sales of which may be in excess of $1 billion.

Boyd Lund is pipetting a sample of reaction mixture solution in order to prepare it for analytical analysis.

The premier product of CyDex, called Captisol®, was the brainchild of researchers at the University of Kansas Higuchi Biosciences Center. Captisol is a doughnut-shaped molecule that improves the solubility of certain drugs by attracting and holding an insoluble ingredient in its center, making the entire complex water-soluble. This technology allows patients to absorb the medicine more readily into their bloodstream.

Pfizer, Inc. has licensed Captisol from CyDex for two important new treatments now moving through the regulatory process. In September 2000, Pfizer received its first regulatory approval in Sweden for an injectable medicine with Captisol to treat patients suffering from schizophrenia. The schizophrenia compound is now under regulatory consideration in major markets. CyDex also is collaborating with Pfizer on a proposed new drug for treatment of fungal infections, again using Captisol technology.

In addition, CyDex is partnering with Bristol-Myers Squibb, Daiichi, PTC Pharma AG, and Allergan on a variety of drugs under development. More than 150 pharmaceutical and biotech firms have evaluation agreements with CyDex to investigate potential uses of its technology.

The future of CyDex looks very promising, said President and Chief Executive Officer Peter Higuchi. The privately held company has added an on-site laboratory, doubled the number of associates, and taken steps to expand existing and new technologies and research capabilities.

Left to right in chairs: Gerold L. Mosher, Ph.D., Director, Product Development; Susan M. Gardner, JD, Vice President and General Counsel; Douglas B. Hecker, Director, Operations; J. Nita Cogburn, Ph.D., Manager, Product Development; Peter T. Higuchi, President and Chief Executive Officer; Left to right standing:Manda Buff, Materials Management Coordinator; Lorraine Groves, Accounting, Marketing and Media Specialist; Jennifer Kalma, Administrative Assistant, Research and Development; Nancy Oelschlaeger, Corporate Executive Assistant; Boyd M. Lund, Manager, Quality Assurance and Quality Control; Rebecca Wedel, Research and Development Intern; Thomas F. Krol, PharmD., Director, Corporate Development; Karen Johnson, Research Scientist; Diane O. Thompson, Ph.D., Sr. Vice President, Research and Development

Doug Hecker is monitoring Captisol inventory in the main storeroom.

The company's revenue grew at a rate of 822 percent in its first five years. Higuchi said CyDex associates share in the success of the drug delivery company.

"I am very pleased and proud of the accomplishments we have made to date—as a team, we are creating our own growth," Higuchi said. "It is a little more difficult growing a life sciences company in the Midwest, away from the clusters of activity on either coast. But the people and knowledge base we have in Kansas City offer a wonderful, mostly unrecognized resource to companies like ours that are built on scientific innovation."

As Kansas City makes a concerted effort to increase the area's involvement in life sciences research and related industries, CyDex has become a pacesetter as a firm that already has established a track record in commercializing new technologies.

CyDex has put in place the major pieces for an emerging company: an experienced management team, research and development scientists and laboratories, technologies that add value to pharmaceutical products, and alliances with major global players.

Just as the Kansas City life sciences initiative and its collaborative partnerships have big dreams for human health care, so does CyDex. Higuchi envisions the region's life sciences research creating future opportunities for CyDex to advance the development of new drugs, but he emphasizes that the fruits of those efforts are still years away.

"You won't have the wealth creation that research laboratories can bring without effective commercial development based on the discoveries from those labs," Higuchi said. "If Kansas City wants to be a player in the life sciences arena, then we're going to have to translate early-stage research and funding into commercialization that turns this research into products that are useful in the marketplace. That's the long-term challenge."

Higuchi said CyDex is currently expanding the applications of its technology into additional routes of drug administration, from oral delivery in the form of tablets and liquids, to drugs that are delivered into the respiratory tract by way of inhalers.

"We are also applying our technology to a number of off-patent and soon to be off-patent drugs, with the goal of creating new and improved versions of these products," said Higuchi. "And we are evaluating additional technologies that would expand our offerings as far as drug delivery systems go."

A benefit of improved drug delivery systems is increased simplicity in the patient's dosing regimen, which can reduce side effects and adverse physical reactions while improving the patient's ability and willingness to take the medicine. When a patient is required to take multiple pills or take them many times through the day and night, the regimen becomes tedious. A new formulation can greatly enhance the experience.

CyDex also is working to bring to market a delivery system that moderates the pH levels of formulations in order to lessen the irritation at the site of injectable medications.

In addition, CyDex markets its technology to facilitate life sciences research. A CyDex product called Advasep® is a resolving agent that allows scientists to distinguish between two similar compounds. CyDex has been marketing Advasep since 1996.

With more than 16 years of industry experience, Higuchi has served in licensing and corporate development for Marion Laboratories, was associated with Touche Ross & Co. for several years, and was president of Higuchi & Co., engaged in the areas of corporate finance, technology transfer, and business development.

Higuchi serves on the boards of directors of several companies and civic organizations. He has a B.A. degree from the University of Kansas, a J.D. from Washburn University School of Law, and an M.I.M. from American Graduate School of Internal Management. ▨

Karen Johnson is loading Captisol into the freeze dryer unit.

Mid America Health

One of Kansas City's best known and most trusted health plans, HealthNet, introduced a new name to its customers in January 2002. Changing "only" its name, Mid America Health is HealthNet in every aspect of its business operation. Managed care services are provided to over 5,000 employers through a variety of HMO-based health plans and a PPO network.

Mid America Health focuses almost exclusively on serving Kansas City-based employers and health plan consumers. Over 330,000 members are enrolled. Thriving in what has been defined as the most competitive managed care market in the United States, Mid America Health has realized aggressive commercial growth in its HMO product lines that is unprecedented in this market. The Medicare HMO, Senior Excel, achieved the lead position in the Kansas City area in mid-2001, out pacing long-term competitors by enrolling more than 21,000 individuals in just five years. Company annual revenues have increased correspondingly; jumping from just $10 million in 1995 to projected totals of more than $260 million at the end of 2001.

Mid America Health benefits from distinctive market advantages. A long-term relationship with Kansas City's preferred hospitals and physicians, a reputation for responding quickly to the changing needs of employers, and a commitment to delivering personalized, locally based services form the foundation of a strong market position and consumer appeal. Customized medical

Dr. George Pagels, M.D., president and CEO, and Carolyn Adair, chief marketing officer, discuss Mid America Health's strategic planning process vital to the long-term success of the company. Photo by Ron Berg Photography

management strategies and cutting-edge technology allow the organization to position itself for future growth. The company recently implemented the Erisco Facets transaction system. This flexible, open-architecture computer system is capable of administering multiple plan designs on up to six million people. The system also allows for improved customer service, faster processing of claims, and more targeted medical management to meet member health needs. Over 2.3 million claims were processed on this system in 2001 for all lines of business.

Frequent face-to-face communication with customers is critical to successfully developing products and services that members desire. Medicare HMO members, the Senior Excel Ambassadors, meet regularly to share their insight into issues regarding health care and health plan services with plan leadership. This volunteer group now numbers over 40 enrollees who actively represent their peers in discussions of benefit design, escalating health-care and prescription costs, and access to quality health-care services. Similar activities occur with other segments of the market.

The locally owned health-care company is also in tune with e-commerce demands and recently completed a new consumer-focused Web site that is both interactive and informative. The Web site is colorful, user-friendly, and

The Mid America Health logo, represented in this art glass creation, has become one of Kansas City's most recognizable "hometown" corporate symbols. Photo by Ron Berg Photography

Callers or visitors to Mid America Health can count on a cheerful greeting from Marisa Wates, whose daily mission, she says, is "to make the public's first impression of the company a good one." Photo by Ron Berg Photography

provides members access to the health plan 24-hours a day. The Web site offers members, employers, and providers the opportunity to access the provider directory, reference benefit and eligibility information, and communicate with customer services.

Mid America Health also partners with St. Luke's-Shawnee Mission Health System in offering the Mid America Health Line, a 24-hour telephonic service members may use to obtain medical advice and health information provided by registered nurses. Physician referral services are also available.

Initially operational in mid-1984, Mid America Health first served the Bi-State region for over 10 years as a Preferred Provider Organization or PPO. Partnerships with insurers, large employers, and third party administrators allowed this managed care plan to grow rapidly and establish a highly respected brand image.

A merger with a start up HMO in 1994 turned the company's direction strategically toward HMO-based product lines and strengthened its competitive position. True to its original concept of being a provider-owned health plan, Mid America Health is owned by the Saint Luke's Shawnee Mission Health System, Carondelet Health, and Liberty Hospital. A seasoned management team, led by Dr. George Pagels, M.D, directs the company.

"Mid America Health has realized a great history of success by building customer-focused business strategies around its core values—exemplary service, respect for people, quantifiable accountability, and process improvement," stated Dr, Pagels, Mid America Health's president and chief executive officer. "Hard work, talented people, and careful planning make the organization a leader among Kansas City's health plans."

Kansas City area physicians play a key role in developing health-care management strategies for the health plan. Both primary care physicians and specialists serve as advisors in defining care management guidelines and protocols, and in establishing various health programs for members. Mid America Health Board of Directors is in fact led by a well-known community physician, Dr. John Perryman, M.D.

Inherent in the corporate culture is a passion for reinvesting in the Kansas City community, through both financial resources and its people. Mid America Health's 450 employees dedicate monthly fundraising activities to the areas' charitable agencies and causes, while also pledging substantial dollars annually to the United Way. Long-term sponsorships reflect a corporate commitment to the support of family health-care initiatives, which benefit women and children. Even business partnerships have evolved into shared support of key community activities.

Community-based agencies that have selected Mid America Health as their health plan often find financial support and active participation by health plan staff in their fundraising activities. Key corporate sponsorships include Speaking of Women's Health, a benefit for KCPT, the American Heart Associations Heart Health Luncheon, and Jazzoo. ▨

The customer care call center is one of Mid America Health's busiest departments, averaging 8,000 calls a week. Here, representative Darryl Collins researches a question from the office of one of the network physicians. Photo by Ron Berg Photography

Blue Cross and Blue Shield of Kansas City

In today's competitive health benefits industry, Blue Cross and Blue Shield of Kansas City knows that first impressions are more important than ever.

Blue Cross and Blue Shield of Kansas City is the largest provider of health plans in a 32-county area serving greater Kansas City and northwest Missouri. The company offers a number of benefit programs that can be included in many group health plans for area employers, small businesses, and self-employed individuals.

To bolster strength and gain momentum for the 21st century, Blue Cross and Blue Shield of Kansas City implemented an aggressive initiative to overhaul, consolidate, and improve existing facilities, equipment, and technology. Those offices are located in two buildings downtown at 2300 and 2301 Main, next to Union Station. Under Blue Plan, employees now work in upgraded workstations with state-of-the-art equipment and technology, have access to a new fitness center, and, best of all, enjoy an environment that fosters teamwork and communication.

Tom Bowser is president and CEO of Blue Cross and Blue Shield of Kansas City. Bowser has worked in the Blue Cross and Blue Shield of Kansas City system for 30 years; 20 years in the Kansas City region. "The next few years will be a time of continuing change for the healthcare industry, and no doubt for Blue Cross and Blue Shield of Kansas City," Bowser said. "Our workforce is ready to work together to meet these challenges. We continue to look for ways to enhance the delivery of our products as well as improve our member services."

Blue Cross and Blue Shield of Kansas City has more than 800,000 customers who choose from a comprehensive range of group and individual insurance products. A leader in the development of innovative managed-care programs, Blue Cross and Blue Shield of Kansas City offers two health maintenance organizations, two preferred provider organizations, a dental preferred provider organization, several Medicare supplemental plans, and a Medicaid managed-care program. Total company revenue in 2000 was $713.9 million, the largest increase in the company's history.

Tom Bowser, president and chief executive officer of Blue Cross and Blue Shield of Kansas City.

BCBSKC continues to be the largest health benefits provider in the greater Kansas City area by recognizing customer concerns and crafting insightful business strategies. Employee teams work together to design innovative tools to deliver superior service for the company's members.

The mission of Blue Cross and Blue Shield of Kansas City is to: "Use our role as the leading health insurer to improve the health of the communities we serve."

Blue Cross and Blue Shield of Kansas City has maintained its position as the region's largest provider of comprehensive health benefits for two reasons—by recognizing customer concerns and by crafting insightful business strategies that address those needs.

The Internet-era has brought with it a constant demand for information. This is especially true in the health benefit industry. Customers want immediate access to personal healthcare information, day and night. Physicians and hospitals require Internet capabilities and systems to file electronic claims. Blue Cross and Blue Shield of Kansas City's Web site offers members, employers, and providers the opportunity to access the provider directory, change primary care physicians, check claims status, view premium invoices, reference benefit and eligibility information, and contact customer service. These services are available online 24 hours a day.

Blue Cross and Blue Shield of Kansas City contributes to more than 250 organizations and charities with a special interest in helping children. Monetary donations in 2001 were made to such charities as Juvenile Diabetes Foundation, Rainbow Center for Children, the Lighthouse Preschool, and the Rehabilitation Institute.

With a belief in revitalizing the urban core of Kansas City, Blue Cross and Blue Shield of Kansas City has contributed to the 18th and Vine Jazz District redevelopment project, Science City at Union Station, and the Discovery Center.

While some of the community contributions are financial, others involve volunteer participation in community events and programs. Hundreds of employees walked and ran to help raise money for children and health-related charities.

Through the Kansas City Business Partnership Program, Blue Cross and Blue Shield of Kansas City employees buddy up with students, act as pen pals, or spend time as Junior Achievement instructors. At other times, involvement comes in the form of leadership with many Blue Cross and Blue Shield of Kansas City employees serving in leadership roles at the Hallmark Community Board, the Greater Kansas City Chamber of Commerce, the Tax Increment Financing Committee, Science City at Union Station, and Starlight Theatre.

BCBSKC strives for high service level achievement. By converting to Facets, a single system utilizing the latest technology, our claims, membership services, and customer service representatives are able to more effectively meet customer needs. With the continuous effort on improvement over the past year, BCBSKC hit a 30-year milestone in processing claims. Improvement of service levels will continue to be significant priorities.

The Chamber CHOICE program, created in 1994 through a partnership with the Greater Kansas City Chamber of Commerce, is now expanded to small businesses with fewer than 25 employees. Since the program's inception, 11 other local chambers have endorsed the program.

As the marketplace continues to move away from tightly managed plans, more members are seeking products offering value-choice options. The Preferred-Care and Preferred-Care Blue PPO plans and Blue-Care HMO allow members to see any specialist within the network of providers without a referral. These plans are growing at a substantial rate.

Blue Cross and Blue Shield of Kansas City has recently completed a conversion of its comprehensive computer system to Facets. Facets has led to an improved level of customer service, faster processing of claims, and a single database that can more accurately analyze trends and set and predict rates. The system also provides physicians and hospitals with increased access to information.

BCBSKC places an increasing emphasis on its accreditation and performance standards and processes. While its quality management department spearheads these efforts, the company is educating every employee of their role in helping to achieve successful accreditation. The company has also implemented several quality programs to improve service and awareness on vital healthcare issues, such as its Preventive Health Guidelines and Disease State Management Programs.

KU Med

At the heart of the 50-acre shared KUMC campus is KU Med, Kansas' premier academic medical center. KU Med is recognized as a leader in patient-centered care and is known for its excellent physicians, nurses and staff, who are specialized and experienced in every aspect of medical care.

The hospital was founded in 1905, but KU Med is just three years old. In 1998, the State of Kansas created the University of Kansas Hospital Authority. This new governing structure allowed the hospital to stay competitive and flexible in today's health care marketplace. The Hospital Authority board is comprised of 14 members who are appointed by the Governor and represent the people of Kansas.

Since its inception, KU Med remains committed to putting the patient first. That is why the medical center stays on the cutting edge of medical care, treatment, and diagnosis.

KU Med has a rare PET (Positron Emission Tomography) Scanner, which permits whole-body imaging to enhance diagnostic capabilities in oncology and cardiology. Men and women facing cancer expect and find the most advanced level of care at KU Med. Patients living with cancer receive much of their care as outpatients at the KU Med Cancer Center, which is staffed and open 24 hours a day.

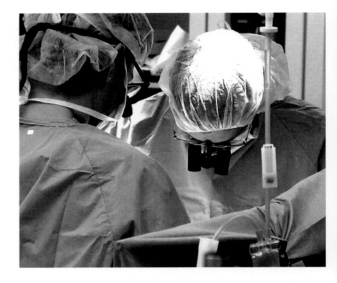

Cardiovascular surgeons at KU Med use the latest procedures and technology.

In addition, the Comprehensive Breast Cancer Center offers screening, prevention, diagnostics, risk and genetic counseling, and treatment. KU Med also recently opened the Prostate Center, where a patient is able to receive care, advice, and treatment from a multidisciplinary team, all at one location.

Patients travel from across the Midwest to see KU Med's neurosurgeons and neurologists, who treat brain disorders such as Parkinson's disease, Alzheimer's disease and epilepsy. This highly qualified and dedicated team of physicians is nationally known for being among the first to perfect an implant procedure for the surgical treatment of Parkinson's disease.

Since performing the area's first successful kidney transplant more than 30 years ago, and the first liver transplant more than 10 years ago, KU Med continues to be a leader in organ transplantation. Transplant patients choose KU Med because the program has one of the best survival rates—as well as one of the shortest waiting lists—in the country.

As a leader in medical care, KU Med has established a new world-class heart and lung program. This program combines two of the most prominent cardiac care groups in the region, offering diagnosis and care of heart disease, cardiovascular surgical expertise, the most innovative medical research, and a commitment to teach the next generation of cardiologists.

KU Med is the region's premier academic medical center.

Samuel U. Rodgers Community Health Center

For over three decades Samuel U. Rodgers Community Health Center has been a cornerstone of Kansas City's health care safety net. Located just east of downtown, Rodgers Health Center was founded on the principles of increasing access and eliminating barriers to health care. Rodgers Health Center has given hope for a healthy future to thousands of children and families.

"The final test of a leader is that he leaves behind him in other men the conviction and the will to carry on."—Walter Lippman

One Man's Vision

In 1968, Samuel U. Rodgers, MD, MPH, opened a health center in Kansas City, with the dream to take care of poor people, treat them with compassion, and make their lives a little easier. Dr. Rodgers created a health center that would do more—one that would make health care available regardless of a patient's ability to pay, educate people about their illnesses, and teach them how to remain well. The health center that began as one man's vision is now a shining example of how one person can make a difference. Samuel U. Rodgers Community Health Center stands proudly today in his honor.

One Health Center and a Mission

Samuel U. Rodgers Community Health Center delivers comprehensive services including adult and pediatric medicine, women's health, dentistry, and mental health care. Rodgers incorporates an adult day care center, patient transportation, pharmacy, community health outreach programs, the women, infant, and children (WIC) nutrition program, and interpreter services to bring care to all.

Rodgers Health Center is a leader in designing community-responsive programs:

- In 1984, Rodgers established the Quality Care Center at Northeast High School to address student health concerns with emphasis on reducing teen pregnancy (and corresponding student drop-out rate). In the 1990s, Rodgers opened four more school-based health centers.
- In 1985, Rodgers, partnering with local leaders, initiated an annual citywide health fair that features free health screenings and health education in a festival setting.
- In 1990, Rodgers South, a substance abuse treatment program, opened. Today, the center serves over 200 clients monthly.
- Rodgers employs interpreters and health care professionals who are fluent in many languages to serve the 42 percent of its patients who are non-English speaking.
- In 2000, Rodgers launched nurse mid-wifery care to provide culturally sensitive care to women from around the world.
- In 2001, Rodgers opened its newest location, Rodgers-Lafayette Community Health Center, in Lexington, Missouri, to serve rural families.
- Today, with 180 staff persons in 11 locations, Rodgers serves over 17,000 patients each year.

Volunteers at the annual health fair carry on the legacy of providing health care for all.

13

Chapter Thirteen

HIGH TECHNOLOGY, MANUFACTURING & DISTRIBUTION

Butler Manufacturing Company

Butler Manufacturing Co. maintains a century-old tradition of fabricating quality steel products that led to the company's present dominance in pre-engineered metal building systems.

Butler originated in 1901 when three men in Clay Center, Kansas, envisioned a market for galvanized steel livestock tanks. Charles Butler, his brother Newton and friend Emanuel Norquist pooled their vision and capital to launch a company that they located in Kansas City, Missouri. Over the years, Butler fabricated a diverse line of products ranging from residential garages, pails, and biplanes to railroad tankcars, grain bins, and metal buildings. If a product involved bending, roll forming, and welding steel, Butler had the expertise to mass produce it.

The company was exploring the potential of mass-producing rigid frame structural framing when the outbreak of World War II deferred the idea. Butler spent the war years fabricating a variety of war material, including another version of metal building needed for aircraft hangars, barracks, and support facilities. When the war ended, the company began selling off a stockpile of surplus metal buildings left from canceled government contracts. Butler soon developed a dealer organization to sell and erect them. That network of Butler Builders® today numbers more than 1,200 affiliated general contractors that give Butler nationwide reach into virtually every local construction market.

Butler had exported buildings and grain bins for nearly 50 years when management was led to make it a truly global company during the 1990s. Business units established since include Butler Shanghai, Inc., in China; Butler Europe Kft, in Hungary; and joint ventures, a licensee, and manufacturing alliances in Saudi Arabia, Japan, and Mexico. These operations focus largely on regional markets with their own engineering, sales, and contracting resources.

Butler Shanghai, Inc., the company's wholly owned Chinese subsidiary, operates from this new, multi-story headquarters building adjacent to recently expanded plant operations. The Kansas City-based corporation has grown into a global company with other major plants in Hungary and Saudi Arabia.

"We initially served the international markets through export sales but followed our global customers into new markets as they expanded internationally during the 1990s," recounts Don Pratt, Butler chairman. "Each market where we established a permanent presence was carefully assessed for its opportunities and generally required a different business structure to address commercial practices, legal, tax, and tariff issues. In some countries we operate as a wholly owned venture, whereas others are best suited for joint ventures. In still others we have licensed our technology to local entities."

Butler recently completed a new, $24 million headquarters in the historic West Bottoms District of Kansas City, Missouri. The company's commitment has been praised as the needed cornerstone to attract additional building projects into the area. The new headquarters will showcase the most advanced alternatives in building systems for a two-story office building application.

Butler revenues from all operations now approach nearly $1 billion. The largest contributor remains the

Butler hosted a 100th Anniversary party in 2001 at the American royal Building, one of many Butler Buildings in the Kansas City area. The event was attended by current associates, retirees, and many other guests, followed by local celebrations at various plant sites around the world.

buildings division, which produces pre-engineered metal building systems. The products consist of factory-produced structural framing, metal roof systems, metal wall panels, and related subsystems that erect fast and efficiently into a fully integrated structure with more predictable quality.

The Vitsawall Group, which designs, manufacturers, and markets extruded aluminum storefront, curtain wall, skylights, and window systems, has emerged as the company's fastest growing and second-largest business unit. Products from this division have been applied to the current renovation of the Pentagon, a four-acre skylight at the Opryland Hotel, and the replacement skylight for Frank Lloyd Wright's famed Guggenheim Museum. Projects in the Kansas City area include the Stowers Institute, Menorah Medical Center South, the Kauffman Foundation, the Federal EPA Building in Kansas City, Kansas, and the FBI Regional Office.

"Vistawall has clearly been our most successful acquisition," Pratt said as he approached retirement last year after a 37-year career with the company. "We started by acquiring Howmet Architectural Products in 1984 when it was a relatively small business. Butler inherited a superb management team that we supported with strategic product acquisitions and investment in additional manufacturing capacity necessary to achieve steady growth. Vistawall today ranks second, behind a much older company, in their industry."

The Lester Buildings division designs and produces wood-frame buildings for farm and light-commercial uses.

The new World Headquarters for the Butler Manufacturing Company was completed during the company's 100th Anniversary year and showcases many building systems and architectural products for office facilities construction. (Insert photo left to right) Don Pratt, Chairman; John Holland, President and CEO; and Ron Rutledge, Executive Vice President, are shown reviewing plans as the project neared completion.

Some 400 dealer-contractors serve those markets primarily east of the Rocky Mountains. More recently, Butler established Liberty Building Systems to manufacture and directly market a lower-cost line of preengineered metal buildings. Other complementary operations include Butler Construction Services, a corporate construction subsidiary that primarily serves companies with ongoing, multi-site building programs or large, complex structures. Butler Real Estate adds yet another dimension by supporting Butler Builders with financially sound clients that want to lease facilities developed on a build-to-suit basis.

"We will continue to be an innovator," predicts John Holland, president and CEO. "Our core businesses are all complementary and play off our expertise, whether it is a value-priced Liberty Building, custom window and skylight systems, or turnkey construction and development services."

Butler worldwide employs more than 5,000 personnel, approximately 500 of them in Kansas City, Missouri. Training, leadership development, and benefits programs are recognized as the best available for career individuals.

"I travel and visit with our customers throughout the world, and, while we have superb products and technology, those are meaningless unless an organization is supported by dedicated employees," Holland said. "Our focus remains on satisfying each individual customer, but our people determine the ongoing corporate success."

The Vistawall Group supplied window, door, and skylight systems for the construction of Stowers Institute for Medical Research. The most successful acquisition in Butler history, Vistawall has headquarters offices and a large plant in Terrell, Texas. A new aluminum extrusion plant was completed last year in Greeneville, Tennessee to keep pace with growing demand for its products.

Yellow Corporation

After decades spent cautiously building a business by the book, Overland Park, Kansas-based Yellow Corporation is now pulling out all the stops in a race to widen its leadership position in regional, national, and international transportation services.

Yellow Corp. is approaching about $4 billion in revenues and has about 32,000 employees. Its portfolio of companies provides transportation and related services that are global in scope.

Just about anyone who makes a product, or component, or who is involved in the distribution of those products is a customer of Yellow. In fact, on any given day, the Yellow Corporation companies are doing business with about a half-a-million customers—which means that the one-size-fits-all trucking service of yesterday is no longer acceptable.

The transportation industry is shifting to highly reliable, time-definite service that may involve trucks, rail, aircraft, or ocean vessel. Yellow Freight System, the largest operating company within the Yellow Corporation portfolio, today offers a range of services geared to meet these rapidly evolving demands. Innovative, leading-edge technology has helped the company leap ahead of its business rivals.

Yellow Freight moves more than 14 million shipments annually, throughout North America.

Yellow Freight was one of the companies that helped deliver the highly secretive fourth book in the continuing Harry Potter series to dealers, which required precise scope, detail, and execution. The Scholastic team worked alongside Yellow associates and moved the shipments via Exact Express, a time-definite, expedited air and ground delivery service with the industry's only 100 percent satisfaction guarantee. With Yellow on board, the books were shipped directly to destination cities without stopping at a distribution center.

"Our customers keep asking us to do more, and we have to meet that request," said Bill Zollars, chairman, president, and CEO of Yellow Corporation. "Most of our customers are experiencing the phenomenon of shorter and shorter product life cycles. You had better get it on the shelf or get it on the World Wide Web while the window's open because the window is getting shorter all the time."

Yellow is a 76-year-old company that got its start in the oil fields of Oklahoma by two brothers, A. J. and Cleve Harrell. During the 1930s, when the trucking industry became heavily regulated, Yellow expanded its route system to Kansas, Missouri, Illinois, Texas, and New Mexico. Yellow has grown steadily through the years and became a national carrier in the 1970s. The industry was deregulated in the 1980s and '90s, which forced Yellow to become more responsive to market demands.

In 1996, as part of a leadership transition, Yellow reshaped the entire management and organizational structure. The goal was to move decision-making authority closer to the customer and get more people involved in bringing innovative ideas to the table.

One key outcome was the dramatic improvement of service quality on nearly all city-to-city shipping lanes nationwide. In fact, a range of operational process

Yellow Freight driver, Charles Renfroe is one of 23,000 employees who have transformed the company into the industry's service leader.

improvements allowed Yellow Freight to become the first transportation services company to meet stringent new ISO 9001:2000 standards for certification.

Perhaps the Fortune 500 company's most unique feature is Yellow Technologies, whose sole job is to keep Yellow on the cutting edge of technological advances. The company's core purpose—"making global commerce work by connecting people, places and information"—very much depends on its technology leadership.

The company's technology strategy includes the start up and development of *Transportation.com*, a non-asset-based global logistics company that delivers its services through best-in-class Internet technology. Introduced in June 2000, *Transportation.com* utilizes the Internet to provide broad-based transportation and global logistics services to shippers and carriers.

"With the consolidation that is occurring rapidly, *Transportation.com* has become the service leader in this very specialized and exciting market segment," Zollars said.

The shipping industry has embraced time-definite, defect-free transportation, and Yellow has been a leader in defining those new expectations. While the company's transportation assets will always be important, it is information that delivers a sustainable competitive advantage.

Yellow Freight equipment and drivers help keep American commerce moving.

"Worldwide transportation leadership means keeping our focus on the customer," Zollars said. "We provide a range of services that do everything the customer needs to create precision and efficiency within their supply chain. It's all about building the service capability and the technology systems to give the customer what he wants."

Yellow trucks have been a part of the Kansas City skyline for more than 50 years.

Kansas City Power & Light

Kansas City Power & Light (KCP&L), a company that began operations in 1882, has realigned under the name of Great Plains Energy Incorporated. The corporate realignment sets the stage for further growth of the company's strengths as a low-cost power producer, an affordable and reliable energy supplier, and a high-growth business developer.

Great Plains Energy serves as a holding company for three operating subsidiaries: Great Plains Power Inc., Kansas City Power & Light Company, and KLT Inc. Great Plains Energy is traded on the New York Stock Exchange under the ticker symbol "GXP."

Great Plains Power Inc. is the unregulated generation company that develops competitive generation for the wholesale market. The company's strategy for potential growth is three-fold: to build out through construction of combustion turbines and a new coal-fired plant of over 700 megawatts at an existing site; to acquire existing independent power producers; and to partner through joint ventures or alliances.

On an average day, KCP&L provides power for thousands of customers including homes, businesses, industries, municipalities, and other utilities. KCP&L services more than a million residents in 24 northwestern Missouri and

One of the first commercial electrical utilities in the country, Kansas City Power & Light (then Kawsmouth Electric Company) began providing electrical energy to customers on May 13, 1882, from its first power house at 8th and Santa Fe.

Kansas counties—a territory of about 4,600 square miles. About two-thirds of total retail kilowatt-hour sales and revenue are from Missouri customers, with the remainder from Kansas consumers. Delivering that power requires 1,700 miles of transmission lines, more than 10,000 miles of overhead distribution lines, and approximately 3,400 miles of underground distribution lines.

KCP&L operates four plant sites with 18 units providing power to its customers and selling into the wholesale market. Approximately 67 percent of the company's power comes from coal-fired plants. Electric sales from these plants make up operating revenues of more than $1 billion.

Hawthorn #5 has the distinction of being the cleanest coal-fired power plant in the United States, an accomplishment noted in the *2001 National Energy Report*. This facility was rebuilt as a state-of-the-art power plant in the record time of 22 months, rather than the industry norm of 36 months.

KLT Inc. pursues high-growth opportunities outside of the utility industry. The company focuses its holdings in three areas: telecommunications; natural gas development and production; and energy management services. The company's telecommunications venture is a fiber-optic network of 20,000

KCP&L is deeply committed to environmental stewardship. Restoring native prairies and forests on the land surrounding the company's generating stations and substations allows the land to regain its natural biodiversity. © 1993 Chuck Kneyse

route miles for secondary and tertiary markets. KLT Gas Inc. is focused on creating value through early stage exploration for unconventional sources of natural gas in coal bed methane. Coal bed methane is an alternative source for conventional natural gas, which is located more easily and is less costly to drill. The company's third high-growth opportunity is through majority ownership of Pittsburgh-based Strategic Energy LLC. Strategic Energy is the leader in objective supply-side energy management services to more than 16,000 commercial and small manufacturing customers, including numerous Fortune 500 companies, school districts, and governmental entities.

Power of Preserving Nature

KCP&L has large tracts of land around its generating stations and smaller tracts around its substations. As an environmental steward, the company finds ways to restore native prairies and forests on the land it owns. The company's efforts in restoring native grasses and wildflowers on land surrounding its Gardner, Kansas, substation resulted in KCP&L receiving the Wildlife Habitat Conservation Award from the Kansas Department of Wildlife and Parks.

Because of its proven environmental track record, KCP&L was invited to become the only private corporation involved in a new project, *Kansas City Wildlands*. The effort's goal is to identify pockets of native habitat in the metropolitan area and eventually restore and manage the remnants of Kansas City's original landscape.

As the centerpiece of KCP&L's Hawthorn generating station, Hawthorn #5 uses the best available control technology (BACT) to dramatically lower air emissions. The generating station is located on the Missouri River about nine miles northeast of downtown Kansas City.

The KCP&L System Control Center is the hub of power operations for the company's service area of almost 5,000 square miles.

The company has had previous success restoring native habitats as a partner in the Blue River Glade project located within the city limits.

An endangered wildflower, the eared false foxglove, also flourishes today thanks to KCP&L's involvement with the Jerry Smith Farm Park in south Kansas City. The flower was holding on in one of the last strongholds in the state—a KCP&L right-of-way. The Missouri Department of Conservation (MDC) asked the company to expand the foxglove's habitat by clearing additional woody vegetation, which was carefully accomplished. One of the largest populations of eared false foxglove in the state of Missouri is now thriving in this KCP&L transmission right-of-way.

In an effort to restore the endangered osprey, several young ospreys were brought to KCP&L's Montrose Generating Station to roost in collaboration with MDC. And a decade ago, the company partnered with Commerce Bank and MDC in a project to return peregrine falcons to the area. A sustainable population now calls the Kansas City area home.

Power of Associates

Mentoring people and seeing them succeed is the goal of Chairman Bernie Beaudoin. Beaudoin's career in the utility industry spans 35 years. To encourage associate participation in non-profit agencies, the company is dedicated to four areas of charitable giving: diversity, environment, youth/education, and civic efforts.

"Associates are the life of our enterprise," Beaudoin pointed out. "They volunteer to lead Boy Scout groups and PTAs. They serve on city councils and non-profit boards. They help out at schools and are active in their churches. Whenever, wherever a need exists, our associates reach out to help meet that need."

The company enthusiastically encourages associates and their family members to give back to the community by participating in a variety of service projects. Some of the most popular activities include Kansas City Harmony, Junior Achievement, United Way Day of Caring, Kansas City Zoo, and YouthFriends.

Although it is among the area's largest employers, Honeywell Federal Manufacturing & Technologies (FM&T) may be Kansas City's best-kept secret when it comes to technology.

As a management and operating contractor for the U.S. Department of Energy's National Nuclear Security Administration (NNSA), Honeywell FM&T employs more than 120 advanced capabilities and technologies in producing unique, high-tech products for the nation's weapons defense system.

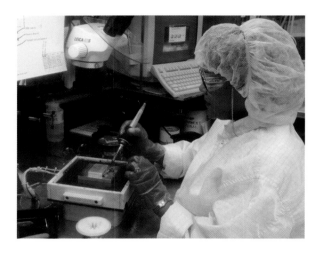

Soldering a cover onto a hybrid microcircuit (HMC) requires a skillful touch by Honeywell FM&T electronic assemblers.

Within the security of the NNSA's Kansas City Plant at 2000 E. Bannister Road, Honeywell engineers, scientists, and technicians support the plant's missions with state-of-the-art production capabilities.

"The Kansas City Plant is a national security asset," says David Douglass, president of Honeywell FM&T. "Our missions contribute not only to our defense, but to the economic well-being of Kansas City, the state of Missouri, and our nation."

Honeywell and its predecessors, AlliedSignal and Bendix, have operated the Kansas City Plant since it opened in 1949.

Honeywell FM&T is backed by the strength of its parent corporation, Honeywell International, a $24 billion diversified technology and manufacturing leader headquartered in Morristown, New Jersey. Honeywell International produces many high-tech products for consumer and government use. Virtually every form of air transportation depends on at least one of Honeywell's systems, including every manned space flight since the beginning of the U.S. space program. Named the "most admired aerospace company" by *Fortune* magazine in 1999 and 2000, Honeywell International employs about 125,000 people in 95 countries.

Technology Leader

Honeywell FM&T is recognized as a leader in science-based manufacturing and high-performance computing. At the center of this program is the Heartland Supercomputer, one of the largest and fastest computers at any manufacturing facility in the world. Using these tools, the company can simulate how a part will hold up in certain conditions or tell manufacturers the most efficient way to build. These techniques provide a better technical understanding of product assembly, reduce development costs and time, and preserve technical information for the future. The Kansas City facility also has one of the largest flexible manufacturing systems in the United States.

The same silicon wafer technology used to fabricate millions of semiconductors on tiny silicon chips is now being used by Honeywell FM&T to fabricate micro-miniature mechanical and optical devices, including motors, transmissions, mirrors, and fluidic devices. The largest gear in these mechanisms is one-half the diameter of a human hair. Potential applications for these micro-electro-mechanical systems (MEMS) range from medical treatment and anti-terrorism to high-speed mirror arrays for Internet optical switching.

Technology Partnerships

The Kansas City Plant continues to spur local economic growth by collaborating with small businesses to the tune of $26 million in transactions during the government's fiscal year 2000. The plant spends $2.7 million annually toward developing technology for commercial applications and providing technical assistance to small-business owners in the Kansas City area.

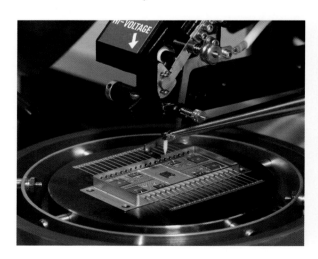

Producing reliable miniature parts is one of Honeywell FM&T's core competencies. On this 2-by-1-inch hybrid micro-circuit (HMC), the one-mil gold wire electrical interconnections are attached by applying heat and ultrasonic energy through the white ceramic bond tool.

The Kansas City Plant features three major complete factories, all under one roof, mechanical, electronic, and engineered materials. In addition to production capabilities, the Kansas City Plant provides laboratory testing and analysis, training program development, and vehicle safeguarding.

Continuous Improvement Culture

Honeywell FM&T is striving to reach the Six Sigma measurement of quality on all products and services. The Six Sigma standard, which represents a 99.99997 percent error-free process, is applied to every function in the Kansas City Plant, from product development to marketing, not just functions on the factory floor.

Honeywell FM&T manages Kansas City Plant operations with the utmost commitment to quality and an unsurpassed dedication to safety. In the 1990s, FM&T became certified to the internationally recognized ISO 9001 quality standard and ISO 14001 environmental management system standard. The plant is also designated a U.S. Department of Energy Voluntary Protection Program STAR Site for its exemplary safety program, and it is a recipient of the Missouri Quality Award.

Community Partner

Honeywell FM&T's contributions to the community are multifaceted and undeniably significant, and the company's more than 3,000 associates are committed to being responsible members of the communities in which they live and work.

With contributions totaling nearly three-quarters of a million dollars annually, Honeywell FM&T is one of Kansas City's largest contributor to United Way. Its associates also participate annually in other local charity efforts

Products produced by Honeywell FM&T undergo extensive laboratory testing. Here, staff engineer Joe Laoruangroch tests a telemeter assembly for acquisition of critical functional and environmental data .

such as Habitat for Humanity, Christmas in October, and Project Warmth. Additional support is given to environmental projects such as the Blue River Cleanup, as well as economic development programs.

Another major area of emphasis is in the classroom. Honeywell FM&T actively supports educational programs and workshops that encourage students to explore math and science. By getting actively involved in these programs, FM&T associates serve as role models for talented young people, helping to promote an interest in math- and science-related careers at an early age.

Each year Honeywell FM&T joins Rockhurst College and the U.S. Energy Department as co-sponsors and hosts of the largest regional Science Bowl in the country. The company and its associates also are actively involved in the Learning Exchange, Science City, and the Society of Automotive Engineers' "A World in Motion" program.

Since 1994, Honeywell and the U.S. Department of Energy have collaborated on the equipment gift program, which allows for the donation of computer equipment and software to area schools.

As a Fortune 50 technology leader, Honeywell is watching out for the next generation of scientists, researchers, and engineers.

To learn more about Honeywell FM&T and the Kansas City Plant, visit the *www.kcp.com* Web site.

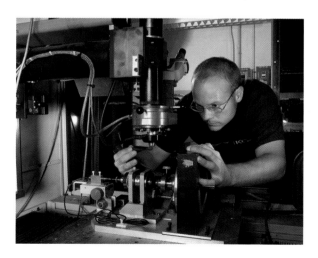

Honeywell FM&T welding operator Danny Fossey performs a laser system setup operation on a CO_2 (carbon dioxide) laser welder at the Kansas City Plant.

John Deere

O ne man's foresight and determination to design and craft quality, efficient equipment caught the attention of hard-working farmers in the mid-1830s. Working in a blacksmith's shop, this man designed the first self-scouring single-bottom plow that efficiently tilled the Northern Illinois soil. He once said, "I will never put my name on a product that does not have in it the best that is in me."

Today, John Deere is one of the oldest businesses in America, and the determination to build high-quality, innovative products with a commitment to farmers is still a major trait of the company.

John Deere recently celebrated 132 years in the Kansas City metropolitan area. The Illinois-based company branched off to Kansas City in 1869. As Kansas City grew so did John Deere. The multinational corporation now conducts business in more than 160 countries and employs 35,500 people worldwide. John Deere is committed to providing genuine value to the company's stakeholders including customers, dealers, shareholders, employees, and communities.

John Deere's 9020-wheeled and 9020-track tractors feature five models ranging from 280- to 450-engine horsepower.

While the leaping deer logo of John Deere has changed eight times in the 165-year history of the company, the concept of being a progressive company remains. John Deere's distinctive green and yellow colors and leaping deer symbol depicts the leadership qualities within the firm that are continually growing within the United States and in the global marketplace.

John Deere products are designed to meet the customers' basic needs: food, shelter, clothing, and transportation. The company is the world's leading producer of agricultural equipment. It is also a major producer of industrial equipment for construction, forestry, and public works markets, as well as lawn and ground care products for homeowners and commercial users. John Deere also provides financial services including credit, insurance, and managed-health-care plans.

Here in Kansas City

More than 250 employees work at John Deere's Agricultural Marketing Center in Lenexa, Kansas. This important hub of John Deere serves as an integrated marketing center, providing market strategy and research, advertising/communications, and employee and dealer training in the United States and throughout the world. The staff also provides branch and dealer retail relationships for more than 1,600 dealers in North America.

Employees often work in teams to identify ways to increase efficiency and productivity. Total benefits from business-process excellence and related activities help to increase market share, gain a better return on assets, and remain extremely customer focused.

John Deere builds tractors for many different work applications. This 5520 is a 45-pto horsepower tractor for small farm, nursery, or commercial operations.

This advanced concept vehicle from John Deere, is an operator-less tractor that is guided by satellite and sensor technology.

The company uses the Global Performance Management Process, in which individual performance and development goals are linked to corporate objectives and are accessible to employees online.

Kansas City was the first sales branch established by John Deere and is now one of seven sales branches in North America. The Kansas City branch serves more than 260 dealers in Illinois, Missouri, Kansas, Nebraska, and the southeastern section of Wyoming.

As the company's second largest distribution depot, Kansas City serves as one of nine depots in the United States. This is important to the dealers because it services all emergency orders with a world-class reputation for parts distribution. Parts ordered by telephone, fax, or computer are shipped at a record pace, usually with less than a 24-hour turnaround.

With three offices in the Kansas City area, John Deere employees find that extra time needed to help others. In fact, collectively, the employee team of Deere raised more than $50,000 to benefit Habitat for Humanity. Then, they actually supplied the labor to construct the project. The employees also are committed to the United Way, donating blood to the American Red Cross and participating in various events held throughout the year to assist local non-profit agencies.

Innovation

From the first self-scouring steel plow in 1837, to a prototype Advanced Concept Vehicle—operated by Global Positioning Systems (GPS)—and high technology sensors, John Deere continues to perfect, create, and construct new equipment.

John Deere spends $1.8 million per day in research and development. Engineers, customers, unions, staffs, and outside suppliers are all involved in the product development process.

The hallmark of John Deere is to build high-quality products that help farmers and equipment operators become more productive in their business and farming operations. The company stands behind the famous saying, "Nothing Runs Like a Deere."

The company is a leader of new products to improve farmer's capabilities and profits. One example is the new 8020 and 8020T series tractors, which offer exclusive features—Independent Link Suspension to get more power to the ground, faster transport and field speeds, and more overall productivity. An industry exclusive ActiveSeat™ offers exceptional operator comfort in the cab, and PowerTech® 8.1 Liter engines deliver a wide constant power range—the 8020 series tractors have significant load capabilities and plenty of engine torque to pull through tough conditions.

The new 9020 and 9020T series, the most complete line of four-wheel-drive and large track tractors in John Deere's history, are designed with wheels or tracks, depending on an operator's needs. In addition, the tractors also offer ActiveSeat™ and an 18-speed PowerShift Transmission.

John Deere's commitment to bring high-quality, productive equipment to its customers will continue to be a major strategy for the future, as they move into new markets around the world.

Harvest at dusk with a John Deere 9650 Combine. A familiar scene in the American heartland.

Farmland Industries

T he Farmland story begins with the producers who work the land. More than 600,000 independent family farmers own the 1,700 local cooperatives that encompass the Farmland Cooperative System. It is these producers and their local cooperatives—in the United States, Canada, and Mexico—that Farmland has been in business to serve since 1929.

Through its partnerships in a cooperative system, Farmland provides the crop production and protection products that help producers use land efficiently. Farmland's feed joint venture provides nutritionally sound animal feeds—from cattle and swine to catfish and horses.

Providing quality products and services that help its member-owners manage their operations is only half the story. At the other end of the food chain, Farmland adds value to its member-owners' grain and livestock.

Through a joint venture, Farmland provides a ready market for the grain grown by its members, which is traded around the world.

The Farmland Cooperative System operates from farm to table and is owned by more than 600,000 independent farmers and ranchers.

From farm to table, Farmland is dedicated to bringing consumers the highest-quality, best-tasting pork, beef, and catfish products. Farmland's long tradition of producing fine foods dates back to 1958. Farmland products can be found in restaurants and grocery stores throughout the United States and in nearly 60 countries. Consumers trust Farmland because it is truly "Proud to be farmer owned.®"

Farmland Is a Partner

The company's asset base includes fertilizer plants in the U.S. and abroad; the largest petroleum refinery in the Midwest; grain elevators; feed mills; beef, pork, and catfish processing plants; and a transportation fleet.

Farmland partners with other companies in more than 60 ventures including; Agriliance, a partnership with Cenex Harvest States and Land O'Lakes that markets and distributes

crop nutrient and ag chemical products; Land O'Lakes Farmland Feed, which manufactures and markets animal health and livestock feed products; and ADM/Farmland, a partnership with the Archer Daniels Midland Company to market grain.

Farmland's Roots

The company was founded in 1929 by six farmer-owned cooperatives that joined forces to buy and distribute petroleum products. It expanded into other co-op products in the early 1930s, and in 1935 changed its name from Union Oil Company to Consumer Cooperative Association (CCA). In 1938, CCA built its first refinery.

By 1939, the Association had grown to include 259 owner-cooperatives and produced more than 200 products. During the late 1950s, the company was a powerful force in agriculture and responded to farmers' demands for more herbicides, insecticides, and other chemicals by purchasing a chemical company in St. Joseph, Missouri.

In August 1966, the cooperative became known as Farmland Industries, Inc. By its 50th anniversary in 1979, it had become the nation's largest farmer-owned cooperative, with its pork processing subsidiary Farmland Foods emerging as one of the nation's leading meat companies.

In 1992, Farmland expanded into the grain and beef business. Today, Farmland functions as a true farm-to-table global agribusiness company, supplying producers with quality agricultural input products, while processing and marketing their grain, pork, beef, and catfish to customers worldwide. Farmland has called Kansas City home since it's founding. ▨

The Farmland brand represents one of the fastest growing food companies in the United States. Our products can be found in restaurants and grocery stores in more than sixty countries.

14

Chapter Fourteen

THE MARKETPLACE, TOURISM & ATTRACTIONS

Chase Suite Hotel

Chase Suite Hotel by Woodfin serves the Kansas City metropolitan area with two "home-away-from-home" locations for business or pleasure, for those travelling alone or with their family. Each suite accommodation has its own landscaped garden entry, separate living areas, and a fully

Our spacious suites have fully equipped kitchens with convenient dining areas.

equipped kitchen. Suites range from one- and two-bedroom studios to two-bedroom penthouses with ceiling fans and cathedral ceilings. With employment trends, especially in the high-tech industry, the all-suite hotel demand remains extremely high and poised to exceed into the 21st century.

Both locations offer 112 suites with 28 penthouses. In addition to complimentary grocery shopping to stock the suite's refrigerator, Chase Suites will shuttle guests within a seven mile radius whether it be to the airport, for shopping, for a meal, or to visit the nearest tourist attraction.

The Chase Suite Hotel at Kansas City International Airport is located just four miles from the airport and within 16 miles of Kansas City's new NASCAR race track, 20 miles from the Truman Sports Complex, only 20 minutes from Union Station and The Country Club Plaza. Just one mile south of the hotel is a myriad of restaurants, shops, grocery stores, night spots, pharmacies, a hospital, and Metro North Mall. The condominium style hotel is situated among the corporate buildings of North Executive Hills, including Farmland Foods, Worldspan, Toyota, ADT, Citicorp, and American Airlines.

The Overland Park Chase Suite Hotel, at 110th and Lamar Avenue just off the College Boulevard corridor in Johnson County, Kansas, underwent a complete renovation in the fall of 1999. It is located just minutes from Sprint's World Headquarters Campus, one block from Black & Veatch headquarters, two blocks from Yellow Freight headquarters, across the street from the new Overland Park Convention Center, Town Center Plaza and Oak Park Mall, several hospitals, and numerous restaurants.

Woodfin Suite Hotels cater to business travelers and families alike. For the business traveler, Chase Suites offer work-smart desks, two-line phones and high-speed Internet access, and 24-hour business centers with complimentary fax, copy, and PC services. Meeting facilities include a conference room to accommodate as many as 50 people with complete catering options available. Two Executive Conference Suites seat up to 10 around a conference table.

Families enjoy the spacious two-bedroom suites with a wood-burning fireplace, two TVs and a VCR, a balcony or patio, and a deluxe kitchenette with refrigerator and microwave. Complimentary grocery shopping service is also available.

Other amenities include free daily continental breakfast, complimentary beverage social hour Monday through Thursday, cable TV with HBO, an outdoor swimming pool, a whirlpool, a gazebo with nearby barbecue grills, and an exercise facility. A coin laundry is on site, and same-day valet service is available.

Family-friendly living room with fireplace and T.V. with HBO.

Corporate suites range from $99 to $169 per night. Extended stays for business travelers are negotiable. Special packages and rates are available for honeymooners, those attending Kansas City Chiefs and Kansas City Royals games, visitors to Worlds of Fun/Oceans of Fun, and for weekends and holidays.

Chase Hotel by Woodfin have locations in Lincoln, Nebraska; Des Moines, Iowa; Fullerton, California; Salt Lake City, Utah; El Paso, Texas; Tampa, Florida; Hunt Valley, Maryland; Baton Rouge, Lousiana; Rockville, Maryland; Dublin, Ohio; and Sunnyvale, Newark, Brea, San Diego, and Cypress, California. There are 18 hotels nationwide, including newly constructed Woodfin Suites in Emeryville, California, just across the bay from San Francisco.

For two years running, Woodfin beat the national occupancy rate by more than 13 percent. Chase Suites corporate surveys show more than a 97 percent approval rating in customer satisfaction. Woodfin Suites has been recognized with high marks in the all-suite category by *Business Travel News*.

Company founder Sam Hardage saw a need for an all-suite hotel concept when he became the first franchisee of Residence Inn, in 1982. Within two years, Hardage founded Woodfin Suite Hotel, the first true second-generation all-suite concept. Hardage, a Wichita native and Harvard Business School graduate, runs the daily operations of Woodfin Suites out of his San Diego office. He's spent the last three decades participating in the real estate industry, owning and presiding over many companies including

Luxuriously furnished bedrooms appeal to both extended stay business travelers and leisure guests.

Hardage Enterprises, Inc., a real estate development, construction, and management company that successfully developed hotels, high-rise office buildings, apartments, and warehouses in six states.

Hardage is an active supporter of a number of professional organizations, private companies, and civic organizations. He serves as chairman of the board of The Vision of Children Foundation, where he holds a personal interest. His son Chase was born with a genetic eye disease, ocular albinism (OA), which causes his eyes to wobble back and forth. The condition typically renders most sufferers legally blind even with corrective lenses. Hardage's son is defying the odds—he attends school, plays soccer, and watches sports.

The goal of the foundation, which has raised donations by selling teddy bears at Chase Suite Hotels by Woodfin, is to eliminate hereditary childhood blindness and vision disorders.

Hardage and his wife, Vivian, reside in California with their children.

Refresh yourself with a quick dip in our pool or relax in our spa.

Helzberg Diamonds

Helzberg Diamonds excels in creating lasting relationships with satisfied customers. Building on the solid business principles with which it began, Helzberg Diamonds offers an exceptional array of fine jewelry and personalized service in a manner that meets today's market.

What began with one storefront in Kansas City, Kansas, has grown into one of the most productive specialty retail businesses in America. With its headquarters firmly planted in Kansas City, Helzberg Diamonds has 236 stores in 34 states. Helzberg Diamonds expects to reach 45 states with an average of 25 to 30 new stores each year for the next five years.

Helzberg Diamonds has increased business through both a 10 percent increase in new locations each year and a natural growth in sales at existing stores as well. In addition to new storefronts, Helzberg Diamonds has also expanded its presence on the Internet with *www.helzberg.com*.

"Whether embracing broad-sweeping trends or celebrating the highest level of customer service…we will continue to be open to change and hope the footsteps we leave will guide future generations," said Jeffrey W. Comment, chairman and chief executive officer.

Diamonds and diamond jewelry fashions have always been the focal point of Helzberg Diamond's merchandising.

A company rich in history

Helzberg Diamonds is a company of many firsts. It was one of the first companies to expand and offer installment payments during the great Depression era. Helzberg's also played an instrumental role in founding the Diamond Council of America, an existing institution that provides jewelers with the science of diamonds and gemology. Helzberg Diamonds was the first local retailer to sponsor a television variety show when television came of age. In later years, the company was among the first to open a location in a covered, suburban shopping mall. In the 1970s, Helzberg's was the first jewelry store to create the "open-store" design, which eliminated all doors and windows.

Morris Helzberg founded the company in 1915, operating a small storefront operation in Kansas City, Kansas. After he suffered a sudden illness, his son Barnett, who was only 14, assumed the top spot at the company. Barnett had big dreams and high hopes for Helzberg Diamonds. By 1948, with Barnett's ingenuity and marketing prowess, Helzberg Diamonds grew into a chain operation with 11 stores in Kansas, Missouri, and Iowa. That was the same year he opened the store of his dreams on the Country Club Plaza. The store was built on three levels and sold fine china and silver in addition to jewelry. Two years later, Barnett showcased the Hope Diamond and the Star of the East at the Plaza location.

Helzberg Diamonds on the Country Club Plaza in Kansas City, Missouri, is brightly lit for the holiday season in the 1940s.

When Barnett stepped up to chairman of the board, giving his son, Barnett Jr., then 29, the responsibility for leading the company, Helzberg operated 39 stores. A few years later, Barnett Jr. fell in love. That feeling turned into Helzberg's largest marketing campaign known simply as the little red buttons with the saying, I AM LOVED®. The notion of wearing a button spread around the world. I AM LOVED® buttons are translated into French, Italian, Spanish, Hebrew, Russian, German, Japanese, and Polish. More than 33 million of the free buttons have been given away.

By 1980, Helzberg Diamonds adopted a merchandise position that focused on diamonds. Fine quality always had been a requisite for the company's jewelry designs, and now fashionable style was made an equally important element. By the mid-1980s Helzberg Diamonds had become one of the most productive jewelers in the country, and rapid growth continued. In 1988 Barnett brought retail leader Jeffrey W. Comment in as president of the family firm. Seven years later, the acquisition of the company by Berkshire Hathaway positioned Helzberg Diamonds for continued growth and strength in the twenty-first century.

The Helzberg Diamonds name carries a long-standing commitment to quality combined with impeccable service. Those standards, which were set forth by the Helzberg family, remain in tact today and will continue to guide the mission of the company into the future.

Jeffrey W. Comment said the company draws strength from its mission statement, "To serve each and every customer in a very special way." "We really take that to heart," Comment said. "If you're going to work with us, you'll build relationships with the customers; that's a given. We have a reputation of being one of the most service-oriented establishments in the retail industry. When you're selling a product like ours, people have to come in and have a good experience."

A leader in the Community

As the Chairman of Helzberg's, Comment recognized long ago that associates who feel good about the company they work for and the products they sell are also more willing to step up and take an active role in their community.

For example, Helzberg Diamonds takes great pride in the fact that in 2000 more than 90 percent of the Kansas City associates made a pledge to the United Way. The company also sponsors programs at Starlight Theatre and is recognized nationwide for its efforts each year in donating the I AM LOVED® bears to children's hospitals throughout the country through its Santa's Gifts Program.

"We like to think of the Helzberg associates as 'Team Helzberg' and we really have worked hard to keep that family feel," Comment said. "As a result, we have come to appreciate over the years that not only do we like to work together to make 'Team Helzberg,' but we find great gratification in giving back to the community both in human services and in the arts."

"We have no grandiose desire to be the biggest," Comment said. "But we always want to be the best in service to our customers, provide a career for our associates, and a great investment for our parent company, Berkshire Hathaway."

An advertisement in 1967 announced the I AM LOVED® campaign. The slogan exists today as an integral part of the company's corporate identity.

Santa (CEO Jeff Comment) brings joy to many children throughout the country with a gift of the cuddly I AM LOVED® signature bear.

Historic Suites of America

Located in the heart of Kansas City, Historic Suites of America combines history and hospitality. Inside, the design is reminiscent of an era gone by with an ornate sculptured skylight that greets guests as they enter the enormous carved-wood rotunda. A brass and wrought iron grand staircase leads guests to perfectly appointed suites. With guests being the number one priority, old-world hospitality is the norm in all three buildings of the refurbished 19-century brick and stone hideaway. One of these three, Kansas City's flagship building, once served as the Builders and Traders Exchange, beginning in 1889. Later, the building evolved into loft space, where Kansas City artists created fine watercolors.

All of the buildings that stand today are completely renovated and are listed on the National Register of Historic Places. The hotel, refurbished with modern conveniences, maintains its historic atmosphere with deeply grained mahogany, wainscoted walls and verdigris ironwork, beveled leaded glass windows, and expansive views of the River Market and Kansas City's affable skyline.

"Kansas City boasts a unique assortment of historic structures," said Carl Galbreath, general manager. "At Historic Suites, we've taken an architecturally rich setting and turned it into an unforgettable guest experience. You will not find another hotel in Kansas City—or for that matter, the world—that contains the architectural attributes found at Historic Suites."

It is the natural architectural beauty combined with soft elegant touches and pampering that make guests feel like they are home away from home. There are 100 suites that feature unique layouts and start at $105. Guests are able to select from 32 different floor plans. Suites range in size from 550 to 1,500 square feet in size. Each room features original architectural features, from skylights and Palladian

Two-bedroom, loft-style, an incredible 1,500 square feet of living space.

windows to 12-foot ceilings and spiral staircases. All bedrooms include either queen or king beds covered with dark blue hues combined with cream and crimson spreads piled high with wonderfully billowy pillows. All come with a complete kitchen. As for in-room ambiance, lofts in many of the suites add a romantic touch, and two on-site whirlpools give sweethearts dual domains for soaking away their cares. Cable televisions in living rooms and bedrooms offer a way to stay connected to the outside world. Guests also receive a complimentary daily copy of *USA Today*.

Packages are available for weekend getaways, Kansas City Chiefs Football Games, March Madness Basketball with the Big XII and NCAA, and of course one- and two-bedroom suite options for honeymooners. This package includes a champagne gift basket, complimentary breakfast buffet, and a late checkout.

For those who want to flex their muscle, Historic Suites of America offers an on-site fitness facility that showcases a variety of exercise equipment, a spa with whirlpool and sauna, and outdoor swimming pool. Also available is a daily breakfast buffet, evening manager's reception—serving complimentary wine, beer, soft drinks, and hors d'oeuvres, and a light dinner served on Wednesdays.

Spacious studio suite, features all the comforts of home including a fully equipped kitchen.

The grand staircase is elegantly decorated for the holidays.

Additional amenities include: one-day dry-cleaning service, on-site laundry, complimentary parking, and phones with data ports.

Of course, the Historic Suites staff also helps ensure the property's ambiance. Always friendly and knowledgeable, Historic Suites personnel can assist visitors with everything from reservations to requests. Guests might seek advice on the area's best restaurants, take the van transportation to nearby businesses or entertainment, or even order their groceries delivered to their kitchen.

Within Walking Distance

Whether on business or enjoying a relaxing weekend away, Historic Suites located at 6th and Central offers both the options of being close to business or relaxing in the hotel. Some of the city's most popular restaurants and nightspots are within minutes. The central location also makes it convenient for business travelers who want to attend events at Kansas City's Convention Center, Barney Allis Plaza and the Music Hall, H. Roe Bartle Hall, and Municipal Auditorium.

Thanks to a combination of turn-of-the-century architectural charm, the latest in hotel and meetings management capabilities, and a professional commitment to service, Historic Suites provides the ideal venue for

small meetings, strategic planning sessions, and more intimate break-out functions.

In addition to being able to hold meetings in the suites, the hotel also offers complete meeting room services, which are perfect for larger gatherings, such as boards of directors meetings or corporate training functions.

The Conference Room is the largest room with 1,750 square feet. It offers conference-style seating for 30 or theater seating for 45. The space includes a public address system and audiovisual equipment on site. In addition, there is a built-in kitchenette equipped with a refrigerator, ice maker, coffee service, and glassware.

For such events as smaller-sized sales groups or networking meetings, the hotel offers the Carriage Room with 775 square feet and room for 30 people. This more casual seating room also has a fully equipped kitchen. The third option is the hotel's 450-square-foot Board Room for smaller parties and groups.

"We regularly host meetings and conference groups ranging from board members to regional sales staffs, and their gatherings all seem to profit from the richness of our surroundings and the ease in which we can accommodate them," said Beth Krizman, director of sales. "The people who meet within our hotel receive our special attention from the moment we begin planning their event until they walk out our front doors."

Comfort and convenience, ease and enjoyment, enormous size and style: Guests find it all at Historic Suites.

One-bedroom suite, featuring uniquely arched windows and wood-beam ceiling.

The Carlsen Center

The Carlsen Center at Johnson County Community College is known worldwide as a cultural arts center that meets the rich and diverse needs of area residents. Well-known entertainers, from Doc Severinsen, Maureen McGovern, and Lou Rawls to the Vienna Choir Boys, London City Opera, Russian National Orchestra, European ballet companies, and many others, have performed on the Carlsen Center stages.

Charles J. Carlsen, who was instrumental in the building's development. Yardley Hall is named for Arthur and Alma Yardley, whose bequest supports performances in the center.

The center celebrated its 10th anniversary in 2001. Headliners for 2001-2002 include the Academy of Ancient Music in an all-Mozart program, a revival of *Strike Up the Band*, and a performance by '60s icon Arlo Guthrie. Special performances families would enjoy include those by Vinok Worldance, performing the music of 30 cultures; Inti-Illumani, an instrumental troupe from Chile; and *The Clown Princes*, ragtime music from the silent film era.

In addition, the college provides an arts education program for children of the community. Last year, more than 5,200 students, ages pre-kindergarten through middle school, from 43 schools in Kansas and 29 in Missouri, attended professional productions in the Carlsen Center.

The Carlsen Center is also home to the Gallery of Art, which presents internationally known artists in all media, ranging from Dale Chihuly's works in glass to Kerry James Marshall's provocative paintings. Located just off the main lobby of the Carlsen Center, the gallery works with artists, museum, galleries, and private collectors to offer seven exhibits each year.

The Gallery of Art is free and open to the public. Tickets to Carlsen Center performances may be purchased through the center's box office. 🔳

Housing both Yardley Hall and The Theatre, the Carlsen Center, home of the Carlsen Center Series, at JCCC is Johnson County's premiere cultural arts center.

What began as a dream of the college's founders 30 years ago has evolved today into a cultural pillar of the Kansas City metropolitan area. The Carlsen Center plays host to more than 250 performances a year and is applauded for its superior acoustics and technical qualities. Guests are greeted with impressive architectural beauty as they enter the center with its three theaters and recital hall, embraced by unusual brick sculptures and an 85-foot-high glass ceiling.

In 1998-99, more than 117,000 people attended events in the Carlsen Center. The center houses the 1,340-seat Yardley Hall, a 400-seat Theatre, a small Recital Hall, and a Black Box theater for student performances. Originally called the Cultural Education Center, the Carlsen Center was renamed in 1998 in honor of the college's president,

The Gallery of Art at JCCC brings the work of nationally and internationally renowned contemporary artists to Johnson County.

The Quarterage Hotel

Located in Kansas City's famed Westport Historic District, The Quarterage Hotel mixes tradition with today's contemporary lifestyle. Situated on the old site of what was once the city's first hostelry, The Quarterage Hotel is part of a bustling midtown area filled with unique shops, specialty stores, entertainment, and restaurants.

The hotel's interior boasts a classically elegant foyer of marble, oak, and brass decorated in the Continental tradition. Yet the real differences are not so much in the setting, but in the service and facilities that provide the perfect home-away-from-home for leisure and business travelers. Close to Kansas City's corporate, financial, and convention centers, yet only minutes away from the famed Country Club Plaza shopping district.

With 123 rooms, the hotel has all the intimacy of a European-style bed and breakfast. The complimentary breakfast, available to all guests, is a hearty feast that includes scrambled eggs, potatoes, biscuits and gravy, cereal, fruit, and pastries. Complimentary cocktails are also served in the hospitality lounge.

The tastefully appointed rooms feature two two-line telephones with data ports connected to T-I lines. Special touches include an oversized working desk with swivel executive chair, iron and ironing board, and in-room coffee for convenience.

The executive and honeymoon suites have king beds and offer features such as wet bars, refrigerators, and separate double-sized showers. Additionally, the honeymoon suite package includes breakfast, cocktails, a bottle of wine, and a Jacuzzi big enough for two.

With all these amenities it is no wonder that more than 900 business travelers have taken advantage of the VIP club membership offered here.

"If a guest stays with us 10 nights, they get an additional night free of charge, and we will upgrade our clientele to a suite if it's available at no additional charge," said

The Quarterage conveniently serves Crown Center, The Plaza, and midtown areas. The Quarterage—where business meets pleasure and charm meets value.

Jim Clark, managing partner. "If executives are traveling with family members, spouse and children stay free in the room."

The hotel has five meeting rooms that can accommodate 10 to 100 guests—the perfect setting for small group seminars to corporate presentations.

For the fitness-minded, the hotel offers its guests an on-site dry sauna and whirlpool or a free workout at a nearby full service health club that provides state-of-the-art equipment and a certified massage therapist.

"We offer our guests an exceptional value. Our complimentary breakfast and cocktails, free local calls and access to the guest's long distance carrier, along with free parking keeps our guests happy and returning year after year. A comfortable stay with no surprises, that's our goal," said Clark.

Sophisticated and professional, yet Midwestern-friendly, The Quarterage Hotel is a hometown business that feels a strong obligation to the community. Aside from offering discounted programs and rates for local universities and cultural organizations, the hotel is also a major supporter of the Children's Mercy Hospital and provides special guest room programs for indigent patients through the American Cancer Society.

"Even though we are a small hotel, we feel an obligation to give something back to the community that we are so integrally tied to. Be it in the Westport area, Chamber of Commerce, Convention and Visitor's Bureau, we want to give to them support," said Clark. "Being a part of Kansas City's overall improvement is very important to us."

The restful lobby area captures the hotel's traditional elegance.

AMC Entertainment Inc.

The movie theatre industry as we know it today, complete with stadium-seating megaplexes, high-tech presentation, and a range of movies to suit every taste, has been driven for decades by innovations that came not from Hollywood or the Great White Way, but from Kansas City's own AMC Entertainment Inc.

Building on its 80-plus years of leadership, AMC has grown from its Kansas City roots to become the world's premier theatre circuit. The AMC circuit now consists of 180 theatres with 2,768 screens in North America, Europe, and the Pacific Rim, featuring the industry's largest and most productive portfolio of modern megaplex theatres. More than 150 million moviegoers per year choose AMC Theatres.

"From the multiplex to the megaplex, AMC innovations have changed the moviegoing experience for the entire world," said Peter Brown, chairman and chief executive officer. "Our innovations have sprung from a legacy of intense focus on our moviegoer at every level of our company."

AMC has pioneered virtually every improvement in modern movie exhibition, from the cupholder armrest

AMC's innovative theatre design provides today's moviegoer with stadium seating, comfort, and industry-leading picture and sound.

to the computerized box office and advance ticket purchasing on the Internet. AMC also developed the MovieWatcher® program, the theatre industry's first and largest frequent-moviegoer reward program. More than 3 million moviegoers around the world enjoy the benefits of MovieWatcher membership.

AMC's leadership is in large part the legacy of Stan Durwood, who rejoined his family's small, regional theatre chain up on his return from World War II. From the 1940s until he died in 1999 at age 78, Durwood's innovations earned him a lasting place as a legend of the theatrical exhibition industry.

Since then, AMC has continued to widen its lead in bringing moviegoers the best in seating, sight, sound, comfort, and amenities. Through a winning combination of strategic vision and sound financial planning, AMC has increased its industry-leading market share, and it dominates the Top 50 theatres in North America, holding 48 percent of those positions.

That leadership stems directly from the AMC tradition of innovation and care for the customer. "We see things from our guests' point of view," Brown said, "and I've always thought that attitude gives us a notable advantage in the marketplace." Indeed, that attitude built a company that stands as the acknowledged leader of its industry worldwide—and it all started in Kansas City.

AMC megaplexes are the overwhelming favorite of moviegoers in Kansas City and around the world.

15

Chapter Fifteen

REAL ESTATE, DEVELOPMENT & CONSTRUCTION

J.E. Dunn Construction

I f there is one universal hallmark of every member of the Dunn Family, it is unquestionably this: their integrity is all consuming. From the day that John Ernest Dunn, Sr., founded the J.E. Dunn Construction Company, the family has been committed to doing things right. Theirs has been a unique, familial team environment in which commitment to clients, employees, and community has never faltered.

J.E. Dunn Construction-Kansas City, a member of the J.E. Dunn Group of construction companies, is a commercial general contractor with expertise in construction management, program management and design/build projects. J.E. Dunn is one of the largest construction organizations in the United States with projects in more than 43 states.

Led by company president, Terry Dunn, J.E. Dunn Construction-Kansas City is a construction management expert, one of the first in the nation to develop this construction delivery method. J.E. Dunn offers traditional business values of uncompromising integrity, with the latest in construction innovations. More than 75 percent of J.E. Dunn-Kansas City's business originates from repeat or referral clients. Its team of professionals number well over 1,500 with an additional 1,500 employees located at J.E. Dunn Group company offices throughout the United States.

For almost a century, Union Station has stood at the center of Kansas City as a symbol of its heritage and history. J.E. Dunn restored Union Station to its rightful place in the heart of Kansas City, so its rich heritage will continue to be enjoyed by generations to come.

Kansas Citians have seen the J.E. Dunn name on company cranes and trucks at many construction sites that dot the metropolitan area. Each project has provided its own set of challenges, and for each, the risk-reward ratio has always kept the company squarely focused on its customers' goals.

The J.E. Dunn name is behind a multitude of Kansas City landmarks, from the Community of Christ Temple in Independence, to the American Century Towers I and II near the Country Club Plaza, to the historic renovation for UtiliCorp United of the New York Life building downtown.

Other projects include the Sprint World Headquarters Campus, the largest project of its kind in the nation; the Union Station renovation and Science City; the Stowers Institute for Medical Research; and the Charles Evans Whittaker U.S. Federal Courthouse.

The J.E. Dunn organization has closely held the belief that exceptional performance in these five key areas is necessary for long-term survival in the construction industry: quality, integrity, economy, performance, and safety. Time and again, the unwavering commitment to each benchmark has distinguished J.E. Dunn as a national leader in the construction industry.

"I started out in this business as a builder of buildings," said Terry Dunn, president and CEO, "but I soon learned I had to be a builder of people."

The company's commitment to human capital through expanded training and educational programs has redoubled; programs are ongoing almost daily, with even the most seasoned J.E. Dunn employees learning new and innovative tools for expanded excellence.

At the Stowers Institute for Medical Research, the motto is "Hope for Life." The standards of excellence at this state-of-the-art research facility attract world-class researchers, all working on innovations for hope and for life.

J.E. Dunn was honored to win the U.S. General Services Administration's first ever Honor Award for Construction Excellence for the Charles Evans Whittaker U.S. Federal Courthouse, an all-metric construction project.

In 2001, J.E. Dunn Construction-Kansas City received the Honor Award, the highest award given by the General Services Administration and the first ever given for Construction Excellence. The Honor Award was presented to the company for its work on the Charles Evans Whittaker U.S. Federal Courthouse in Kansas City.

The same steadfast relationship-building foundations that John Ernest Dunn, Sr., founded the company with in 1924 continue today. Ernie Dunn believed that values should form the bedrock of his company. World War II provided many project opportunities for Dunn, but it also provided a means for Dunn to showcase his commitment to integrity. J.E. Dunn Construction completed the Kansas City Quartermaster Depot for the Army Corps of Engineers a month early and under budget. But Ernie Dunn thought it unpatriotic to profit from war, so he asked the Corps to reduce his contract so that the company was paid only job costs—no profit. With this gesture, Ernie Dunn Sr., solidly established his company's reputation for integrity. This legacy of values and integrity has been handed down to the second, third, and fourth generations of Dunns working for the company.

It is these values and relationship building that J.E. Dunn fosters in its commitment to the community and charitable organizations. J.E. Dunn gives of its time and resources to numerous organizations and encourages its employees to get involved, while supporting their efforts.

For the past several years, J.E. Dunn employees have been among the highest per capita givers to the Heart of America United Way. In addition to employee contributions, J.E. Dunn celebrates an ongoing investment goal of 10 percent of its corporate pre-tax earnings into the community through the broadest range of charitable efforts.

"Businesses have both a civic and a moral obligation to give back to the communities that have supported them," said Terry Dunn. "This means demonstrating a commitment that goes beyond the checkbook. Our community needs to know that business cares."

J.E. Dunn has seen its portfolio of projects grow from a regional to a national scope. From hospitals to office facilities, to prisons, and educational facilities, the list of projects is as diverse as can be found anywhere in the U.S. With less than $150 million in revenues in 1991 to more than $1.5 billion in 2001, J.E. Dunn is one of the largest and fastest growing construction organizations in the United States.

Each day, the 15,000 Sprint employees who work at the Sprint World Headquarters Campus, the largest single office project ever built in the U.S., enjoy the benefits of this total campus atmosphere.

Fogel-Anderson Construction Co.

Fogel-Anderson is a company of integrity, financial strength, and stability—a company dedicated to a high-quality end product while always continuing to improve the project delivery system. Most importantly, Fogel-Anderson Construction Co. is a company built on strong client relationships. The company has built and expanded its business by growing with long-time clients as they entered new markets or identified new construction needs.

Hampton Inn, Shawnee, Kansas.

Today, the majority of Fogel-Anderson's business comes from ongoing relationships with clients who have come to depend on the fourth generation Kansas City-based company for highly responsive construction services tailored to their particular needs.

Fogel-Anderson serves primarily Kansas and Missouri locations, but it is also registered to operate in Arizona, Colorado, Illinois, Indiana, Iowa, Oklahoma, and Nebraska, with pending licensing in both Arkansas and South Carolina. The company consistently ranks in the Top Ten among area construction firms, by the *Kansas City Business Journal*.

From motels to office buildings, warehouses to retail power centers, Fogel-Anderson has the experience to transform dreams into bricks and mortar, and make bold corporate strategies a reality. The company offers a full scope of construction and pre-construction services to a wide variety of clients.

As early as the Depression Era, Fogel-Anderson Construction Co. was acting as an Owner's Representative (Construction Manager) for Kansas City Power & Light Company, Standard Oil of New Jersey, several local food processing firms, as well as other clients in commercial and retail businesses. More recently, the company acted as Construction Managers for local and regional developers, food product retailers, state-of-the-art movie theaters, banks, hotels, and individual business owners. Clients include Balls Food Stores (Hen House and Price Chopper) and Cosentino's Food Marts (Price Chopper); Fairfield Inn, Residence Inn & Suites, and Hampton Inn; and Regency Square Shopping Center in Overland Park, Northridge Plaza in Olathe, and shopping centers in Lee's Summit, Independence, and Blue Springs. Fogel-Anderson has been extremely successful in constructing more than 75 Wal-Mart stores and Supercenters and has recently completed two Lowe's Home Improvement facilities in the Kansas City metropolitan area.

Doug Fogel, vice president of business development and pre-construction services, said the company is venturing into the design/build arena.

"This is where the commercial construction industry seems to be headed. Clients are turning to one company to handle the responsibility of designing and building their structures. Buildings today are so complex that it is becoming more efficient and cost-effective to keep everyone under one umbrella. We utilize our wealth of experience to combine the desired aesthetics of design with the budgetary and time requirements of economical construction in a single-responsibility package. We complete the projects on time and within budget on a competitive basis. In the construction process, we base

KCP&L Southland Service Center, Stilwell, Kansas.

our operations on the owner's stated goals and objectives," Fogel said.

Fogel-Anderson maintains a staff of 43 employees that have diverse backgrounds in academics, code enforcement, and engineering, as well as construction. The firm and its staff members have experience throughout the United States, with average annual billings of $40 million.

As Fogel-Anderson continues to develop new markets and new clients, the company has become a leading construction manager in developing Traditional Neighborhood Developments (TNDs). TNDs are sites that include single family, commercial, retail, and multi-family buildings in one development. Fogel-Anderson provides Construction Management for all infrastructure and site development, as well as for the buildings. Among projects under construction in the Fall of 2001 is a 90-acre TND in the Kansas City, Missouri, Northland called Renaissance in the Northland; another TND is Arbor Creek Village, located at 159th Street and Mur-Len Road in Olathe, Kansas. The first phase of this 38-acre project will be completed in the summer of 2002.

Fogel-Anderson has been a leader for more than 70 years in the Associated General Contractors of America, Kansas City Chapter, serving more than 850 member companies in Missouri and Kansas. The company has been active in the Associated Builders & Contractors (ABC) and was recently named ABC General Contractor of the Year for 2000, the first time an ABC member has been so recognized.

Northridge Plaza, Olathe, Kansas.

Company headquarters have been at the same location since 1947—in the heart of the Paseo West Industrial area, providing easy access to all main interstates and thoroughfares.

Martin L. Fogel and his son, Paul Fogel, founded the company in 1915 as Fogel and Son. On January 25, 1917, the company was incorporated and Martin Fogel's other son, Lyle, entered the business. In 1922, Oscar (O. T.) Anderson joined the company. In 1940, Lyle Fogel's son, John Fogel entered the business. Two years later, the company became Fogel Contracting and in 1946 the name changed to Fogel Contractors, Inc. In 1953, O.T. Anderson's son, Ted, joined the firm and later that year, the company purchased Paul Fogel's interest and changed its name to Fogel-Anderson Construction Co. Ted Anderson leads the company as its chief executive officer. On January 31, 1997, Ted Anderson announced the promotion of his son, Phillip D. Bartolotta, to president and chief operating officer. Phillip Bartolotta has had experience with the company for more than 25 years and has worked in nearly every position in the company during that time. On November 30, 1997, Phillip Bartolotta named Douglas Fogel, John Fogel's son, as vice president. 🔲

Mechanical Breakdown Protection, Inc., Lee's Summit, Missouri.

James B. Nutter & Company

A **Roof and a Yellow Flower**
What do a roof and a yellow flower have in common?

They are symbols signifying James B. Nutter & Company to homeowners throughout America. Both carry considerable insight into the way this national mortgage banking leader thinks and acts.

A stylized house rooftop atop a large red "N" is the familiar trademark characterizing the company's invitation to "Come on home" and reminds customers "the best rates are under our roof."

"'Come on home' is one of the nicest things anyone can hear," explains Jim Nutter Sr., who founded the company in 1951. "It's what we're all about. Corny as it may be. Old-fashioned as it may be. Our niche is serving hard-working families—and that has been the key to our longevity."

The second symbol is a yellow flower. A beautiful daffodil, to be exact. To James B. Nutter & Company, this is the symbol of good neighborhoods, of happy places to grow a family. The company has proudly helped neighborhoods grow with mortgages for their homes—all across the United States. But it's much more than that.

A beautiful yellow daffodil is the James B. Nutter & Company symbol of good neighborhoods, a caring reminder of the importance they place on this cornerstone of America's values.

"At the heart of our country's greatness is a strong family in a good neighborhood," Jim Nutter Jr., who joined his father in helping lead the organization in 1984, explained. "We believe in the power of a safe neighborhood, a loving neighborhood where neighbors care about neighbors. We think it's even more important today because, in many parts of many towns, it isn't true anymore—but it can be. If we care enough."

The company has put its money where its heart is. James B. Nutter & Company is still headquartered in midtown Kansas City where the firm began, in a carefully restored, tree-lined area of historic Westport. The neighborhood is affectionately known as "Nutterville" and the houses have been refurbished and painted every color of the rainbow.

Helping America's Neighborhoods Grow

Neighborhoods touched by James B. Nutter & Company can be found in every state in the union. Indeed, it has evolved into one of America's largest privately-owned and operated mortgage banking firms with a portfolio of industry firsts. The company still specializes in single-family home loans and continually looks for new ways to use conventional, FHA, and VA loans to assist today's homebuyer.

"It's a wonderful feeling to go to almost anywhere and see people who say, 'I've had my home loan with James B. Nutter & Company for years,'" noted Jim Nutter Jr. "We derive great satisfaction from having helped three generations of the same family, in many cases, achieve the American dream."

Some good things never change. These 1954 photos show Jim Nutter, Sr. and Bob Evans, Executive Vice President, standing in front of their office. Only three years earlier, they began helping neighbors get low-cost home mortgages. Of course, both Jim and Bob remain active in the company today—even the phone number remains the same!

First in the Nation

As its reputation grew, James B. Nutter & Company earned national recognition for willingly trying new and better approaches to customer service. It was the first company in the United States to close an FHA Senior Citizen Reverse Mortgage, enabling the borrower to receive a monthly payment backed by the equity in her home. And the first in the nation to successfully test and implement Electronic Data Interchange (EDI) with Ginnie Mae. And the first to install EDI quarterly reporting to Ginnie Mae on the mortgage-backed securities program. The firm also ranks first among large mortgage bankers with the fewest mortgage defaults.

In 1995, James B. Nutter & Company became only the third lender in the country to sign a HUD Best Practices Agreement. The agreement formally recognized the company's efforts to promote homeownership among historically underserved borrowers with safe, sound mortgage-lending principles. In 1985, the firm pioneered the True No Cost Refinance Loan and has since closed nearly 100,000 of these loans.

Soul of a Company

Caring about families is the soul of James B. Nutter & Company. It is the belief in the irreplaceable value of strong neighborhoods that drives this commitment. Helping families through community involvement—throughout the nation—is a long-time corporate habit. One of the efforts closest to its heart, however, is the creation of the Sybil Silkwood Nutter Playground just outside Children's Mercy Hospital.

The magical place for young patients—and their families—is a tribute to Jim Nutter Sr.'s mother. Her lifelong commitment to the health center began as a youngster with the donation of a special stained glass window, secured by funds earned from giving plays. The hospital's chapel now displays this sweet gift.

"This is a special commitment that we care very much about," Jim Nutter Jr. said. "It makes all of us feel good—because it is doing good for so many. My grandmother would love it."

"No matter how much our company grows, our roots are in Kansas City, with these people, with these neighborhoods," the younger Nutter concluded. "Fifty years from now, James B. Nutter & Company will very likely be here—in the heart of the city, helping people buy the homes they want." ▨

The familiar "roofed N" marks the national headquarters of one of America's leading privately owned, mortgage banking firms, James B. Nutter & Company.

Both James B. Nutters—Senior and Junior—take pride in helping families all across the United States achieve the American dream of owning a home.

Sheet Metal and Air Conditioning Contractors National Association - Kansas City (SMACNA-KC)

Founded in 1950 with fifteen members, Sheet Metal and Air Conditioning Contractors National Association, (SMACNA) Kansas City chapter was a leader of firsts for the international trade association. They were the first to develop a sheet metal chapter, create an insurance program for its members, conduct labor negotiations within SMACNA, and have a president elected, Harry Basore, Jr., W.C. Wiedenmann & Sons, Inc., to the national organization.

SMACNA-KC represents contractors in industrial, commercial, institutional, and residential heating, ventilating, and air conditioning; architectural sheet metal; industrial sheet metal; kitchen equipment; specialty stainless steel work; manufacturing; siding and decking; testing and balancing; service; and energy management and maintenance. The contractors also provide custom architectural ornamentation such as bronze domes on churches and other metal sculptures, art work, and fixtures.

Above: This steel sculpture was fabricated by using a sophisticated 3-D computer modeling program. A detailed implementation process was used to provide a template to fabricate the sculpture, A. Zahner Company. Below: The exterior work of the Stowers Institute Medical Research included fabricating and installing more than 70,000 sq. ft. of custom stainless steel roofing, 4,000 linear feet of integral stainless soldered gutter, which included 100 downspouts as well as 14,500 sq. ft. of custom built stainless fascia. 17,000 sq. ft. of louvers, 18,000 sq. ft. of aluminum wall panels and various custom handrails, Baker Smith sheet Metal.

The basic concept of SMACNA is to address issues of member firms that impact the industry nationally and internationally. It serves members' needs to improve their competitive advantage and business environment through SMACNA standards, industry education, labor relations, and industry marketing and business studies.

Located in headquarters outside Washington, D.C., SMACNA has 1,908 members in 102 chapters throughout the United States, Canada, Australia, and Brazil. SMACNA is a leader in writing standards, specifications, and guidelines for installations performed throughout the country and abroad. Kansas City's talented contributions to the industry continue with input from a local contractor playing an instrumental role in the creation of the Architectural Sheet Metal Manual—a technical manual that is used by architects, engineers, and contractors worldwide. The American National Standards Institute highly credits SMACNA technical standards, manuals, and guidelines. SMACNA standards and manuals address all facets of the sheet metal industry, from duct construction and installation to air pollution control, from energy recovery to roofing. SMACNA also answers several thousand technical questions annually from architects, engineers, manufacturers, and government personnel.

In the political arena, SMACNA was the first construction industry trade association with a full-time office on Capitol Hill. This office works with congressional committees drafting legislative language and preparing SMACNA members to testify at congressional hearings.

SMACNA Kansas City Chapter is an organization of close to 100 Architectural, Heating, Air Conditioning, and Ventilaton Contractors who employ approximately 1300 Local No. 2 Union Sheet Metal professionals. These contractors design, fabricate, and install exterior and interior architectural work, and HVAC systems throughout Greater Kansas City, the states, Asia, and Europe. They excel in installing and managing jobs on time, within bids, and with the highest standards of excellence and experience. The contractors have attained excellence through an educated and skilled workforce, which is necessary to perform the type of work needed to continue the rapid growth of Greater Kansas City through new construction and the updating and remodeling of the beautiful existing structures that outline our cityscape.

SMACNA-KC has many programs devoted to the art of successful and strategic business management and state-of-the-art building construction. It continuously alerts the contractors to

changes in legislation that might affect them; provides input for codes and correct business procedures; and provides specific management practices for sheet metal contractors. It is also a leader in providing its members with comprehensive year-round safety training, as well as safety publications, videos, and services to assist them in establishing and managing an effective and safe workplace. SMACNA-KC also provides its members with services to help implement their Drug Free Work Place Policy.

Exhaust Systems at the Stowers Cancer Research Center, Cates Sheet Metal Industries.

"SMACNA's role in labor relations and negotiations industry-wide has produced agreements that have served both labor and management very well. The many joint working committees ensure that the labor agreements will be strictly observed and fairly adjudicated." Bill Zahner, of A. Zahner Company said.

"Our partnership with Local Union # 2 is the key to our success. SMACN-KC and Local No.2's focus is always the client, and is heavily influenced by strategies, implementation plans, and mutual goals." Mr. Jerry Schaefer, CEO of Baker Smith and Chairman of SMACNA-KC Board points out.

SMACNA-KC contractors have become more sophisticated as they incorporate the latest in computerized technology, manufacturing, estimating and, the usual office procedures. These contractors have a huge economic impact on Kansas City with nearly 1300 workers.

Every major project in the city includes a SMACNA-KC contractor at some level. In particular, Barnes & Dodge for their work on the Farmland Corporate HQ, Corporate Woods Building 82, Commerce Bank Trust Building, St. Mary's Hospital, and Kansas City International Airport Terminal Remodeling; Baker Smith for their work at Bartle Hall, Stowers Institute, Cathedral Square, Kansas Speedway, and Sprint's World HQ Campus; Cates Industries for their work on the Stowers Institute and 2555 Grand project; Commercial Mechanical for their work on the Environmental Protection Agency Regional Headquarters, Pinnacle Corporate Center, Waterside IV, and Qwest Communications; Environmental Mechanical for Jack Henry Associates, Allied Signal, and Jackson County Vehicle Maintenance Facility; The Fagan Company for their work on the

Butler Manufacturing World HQ, DST Systems World HQ, Utilicorp United World HQ, The Ford Motor Company—MO; The Harton Company for their work on Blue Valley Waste Water Treatment Plant and Blue Spring Hospital; Standard Sheet Metal for their work on the Hoglund Brain Imaging Center and Sprint World HQ Campus; W. C. Wiedenmann for their work on Harley-Davidson Motor Co., O'sullivan Industries, and The Maiman Co.; and A. Zahner for their work at Bartle Hall, many projects in KCMO, and MIT Stata Center—Boston, Disney's Tomorrow Land—Orlando, Millennium Park Project—Chicago, Museum of Science and Industry.

"We will continue to be intimately involved in helping the Greater Kansas City area grow and making our presence known in the 21st century in the cities and states throughout our great nation." Said Mr. Schaefer.

The spiral shape of the RLDA Temple produces a form that could only be constructed using a 3-D analysis. This project changed forever the way designers and fabricators work together. Locating points in space, instead of dimensions, A. Zahner Company

Clarkson Construction Company

Kansas City and much of the Midwest's infrastructure development are synonymous with the talented team that makes up the Clarkson Construction Company, a sixth-generation, family-owned business that plays an integral role in developing and shaping how the city gets from one place to another.

Unified Government's 400-Acre Tourism District.

More than 100 years old, the company began as an excavation company when G.G. (George) Clarkson moved to Kansas City from Kentucky. Today, Clarkson Construction is vertically integrated and does various types of heavy construction work including bridge building, concrete and asphalt paving, grading, water resources management, and energy production work.

Clarkson Construction's services can be broken down into three main categories: transportation, mostly highway and airport construction; site-development for shopping centers and large complexes such as the Kansas City, Kansas/Wyandotte County Unified Government's 400-Acre Tourism District adjacent to the Kansas Speedway; and water-resource construction, which would include dam construction and river modification work.

The firm has been responsible for much of the construction and reconstruction work on many of the area's major interstate highways including I-70, I-29, I-35, I-435, I-470, and I-635, as well as bridges and street systems in Greater Kansas City.

Among its current projects are the first phase of development on the Grandview Triangle reconstruction; the site preparation, utility work, and parking lot and street construction for the Unified Government of Wyandotte County/Kansas City, Kansas, 400-Acre Tourism District; and the 1,700-Acre Shoal Creek Valley Development in Kansas City, Missouri, near Missouri Route 152 and Shoal Creek Parkway. Clarkson Construction crews have also performed considerable work at Kansas City International Airport, Richard's Gebaur, The National Golf Club in Parkville, Missouri, and the Bruce R. Watkins Freeway, including the first and last projects.

In the construction industry, having the latest equipment can be critical in being able to operate at the highest level possible. Clarkson Construction Company's equipment fleet ranks as the largest in the Midwest and is recognized yearly by *Construction Equipment Magazine*.

Clarkson is ranked by the *Engineering News-Record* as the largest transportation and highway contractor in the Midwest, putting in place over $170 million of work in 2000.

Superior Bowen Asphalt Company, which is fifty percent owned by Clarkson, operates seven asphalt plants in the Greater Kansas City Area.

Total Risk Management is a wholly owned subsidiary of Clarkson Construction Company that provides support services to Clarkson's companies in the areas of safety, security, insurance, and human resources.

Clarkson is a contractor that's proud of where it is today, knows where it is headed, and is confident with its place in tomorrow's market. When the construction need is there, Clarkson Construction Company is available to meet it. ▩

Grandview Triangle Reconstruction.

A. L. Huber general contractor

With the celebration of its 100th anniversary approaching in 2003, A.L. Huber will observe a milestone that not many companies reach. This accomplishment is a tribute to the firm's founder, the leadership over the years, and the dedicated staff members who have contributed to the success of A.L. Huber.

Nearly a century ago, August Huber, Sr., a talented clarinet player, found it difficult to earn a living as a musician. To supplement his income, he started a construction business that turned into a career for Huber. And the name A.L. Huber became synonymous with development and building throughout the Kansas City area.

The company has since moved away from residential into all types of commercial and industrial building and restoration of historic structures. A. L. Huber is also one of the leading builders of churches in the Kansas City area, having completed more than 100 such projects.

Today, A.L. Huber is one of the oldest and most respected general contractors in Kansas City, with completed projects throughout the region and around the country. The current leaders of A. L. Huber are the third generation in the business. August L. "Augie" Huber III has been the company's president since 1975. Brothers Joseph and Randy joined the company in the 1970s. Together the three Huber brothers have taken the company beyond the role of a general contractor and offer clients a wide range of services, including hiring design professionals, providing construction management, and general contracting services, as well as help in addressing property ownership and financing issues.

A.L. Huber has grown from the dream of one man into a talented team of 50 highly qualified employees ready to take on the newest challenge. And, Augie Huber is quick to credit the company's employees, for their "tremendous talent and work ethic."

The Commerce Bank Building in Lee's Summit, Missouri is typical of the many commercial projects A.L. Huber has completed in its 100 years in the contracting business.

As to the firm's longevity and success, Augie Huber attributes that primarily to his grandfather's philosophy of focusing on quality and fair treatment of the client. That way of thinking has proved to be good for both the company and its clients. About 75 percent of its projects are repeat business, and many of the company's clients are second- and third-generation customers. Putting quality and fairness ahead of profits is a philosophy that has been reaffirmed by the present generation of Hubers and will serve the company well into the second century of operation.

As A.L. Huber prepares for the next century in business, it combines traditional work ethics while integrating new and innovative ideas.

"Committed to "doing what we say we'll do" is an often spoken phrase. Combining our experience and forward-thinking attitudes provides our clients with well-managed projects, a team that understands maximizing the design, while minimizing the expense, and delivering a finished product better than expected is our specialty," said Augie Huber.

The ultimate goal of A.L. Huber is to exceed the client's expectations, and to build a lifetime relationship.

The Church of the Nativity, a Catholic Church and School in Leawood, Kansas, is one of more than 100 churches A.L. Huber has built in the Kansas City area.

Sheet Metal Workers Local Union No. 2

No matter where residents of Kansas City drive, work, shop, or play, members of Sheet Metal Workers Local Union No. 2 probably had a hand in building it. For 113 years and going strong, the goals then and now are the same; that Sheet Metal Workers make a good, honorable living and are able to retire with dignity.

Members of the Sheet Metal Workers Local Union No.2 possess the training, knowledge, and skills to do every type of sheet metal work with the highest level of craftsmanship. Skills of sheet metal craftsman begin with metalworking and carry over into sophisticated construction applications and craftsmanship. Sheet Metal craftsmen work on everything from family residences, to landmarks such as Bartle Hall, the Sprint Complex, all local hospitals including Children's Mercy, and the Stowers Institute.

Nearly every aspect of local construction involves the shaping of metal from the hands of some 230 apprentices and more than 1,100 highly skilled journeymen. What began as a tinsmith centuries ago has evolved into a highly sophisticated trade that creates amazing architectural sheet metal work in decorations that grace the Kansas City skyline.

The establishment of the Tin, Sheet-Iron, and Cornice Workers' International Association in 1888 by two Kansas City men eventually led to the formation of structural apprentice training programs sponsored by the Sheet Metal International Association.

Two Kansas City men called the first meeting of the International Association of Tin, Sheet-Iron, and Cornice Workers' together in 1888. Archibald Barnes and A.W. Chatfield held the top positions of the Association,

Union Hall of the Sheet Metal Workers Local Union No. 2. 2902 Blue Ridge Boulevard, Kansas City, Missouri 64129.

which eventually led to the Sheet Metal International Association. Seven cities-Toledo, Youngstown, and Dayton, Ohio; Peoria, Illinois; Kansas City, Missouri; Memphis, Tennessee; and Omaha, Nebraska were represented at the first meeting.

Chapters were assigned their designation by drawing numbers from a hat. Kansas City drew number two, so that is how the organization became known locally. Nationally, the union was first known as the Tin, Sheet-Iron, and Cornice Workers' International Association. Over the years, the name changed to become the Amalgamated Sheet Metal Workers' International Association then the Amalgamated Sheet Metal Workers' Alliance and, finally the Sheet Metal Workers' International Association.

One relationship that has remained a key component of how sheet metal workers do business in Kansas City is through membership in Sheet Metal and Air Conditioning Contractors' National Association (SMACNA)-Kansas City Chapter.

"The sheet metal craft is really one that is handed down from generation to generation," said Ken Alexander, Business Representative of Sheet Metal Workers Local Union No. 2. "SMACNA and Local No. 2 work together as a team in the sheet metal industry."

Through successful collective bargaining between Sheet Metal Workers Local No.2 and SMACNA-KC Chapter, funds are provided for 240 hours of classroom training per year of apprenticeship. The training provided to apprentices and journeypersons produce the highest skilled craftsmen in the industry.

Sheet Metal Workers Local Union No. 2 contribute more than $1 million per year for training apprentices and journeymen. Other benefits include health and welfare program, pension that allows for retirement as early as 55 years of age, 401K, contract negotiation, and safety education for its members. Members meet once a month at the Union Hall.

The Union members share in collections for the United Way, participate annually in the Christmas in October program, and Dollars Against Diabetes.

W.C. Wiedenmann Sheet Metal Company, Kansas City, Missouri. Late 1930s.

Photo courtesy of Jim Huffman

16

Chapter Sixteen

UTILITY, TRANSPORTATION &
COMMUNICATIONS

UtiliCorp United

I n May 2001 in its annual review of the region's publicly held companies, the *Kansas City Star* ranked UtiliCorp United at the top of its Star 50 list. The criteria are a combination of size, profitability, growth, and appreciation in market value.

With a decade-and-a-half of aggressive growth under its belt, UtiliCorp scores high on all four. The company today serves utility customers in seven states, two Canadian provinces, Australia, and New Zealand. Its Aquila, Inc., subsidiary (profiled on page 00) is one of the leading wholesale marketers of natural gas and electricity in North America and an innovative provider of risk-management products and services. Aquila also markets energy in the United Kingdom, Germany, and Scandinavia.

UtiliCorp's annual sales were less than $1 billion in 1990. Ten years later in 2000, they were $29 billion and still climbing. More than 90 percent of those 2000 sales were Aquila's, largely from wholesale energy sold to utilities and very large industrial users. UtiliCorp's 2000 earnings before interest and taxes (EBIT) came about equally from U.S. utilities, international utilities, and Aquila.

UtiliCorp spun off 20 percent of Aquila's common stock in an initial public offering in April 2001, but due to a major shift in market conditions later that year, it bought back all those shares in January 2002 by exchanging them for UtiliCorp shares. As a symbol of this recombination, UtiliCorp plans to change its corporate name to Aquila, Inc. in early 2002.

UtiliCorp's 2000 sales placed the company at number 60 on the Fortune 500 list. *Fortune* also ranked UtiliCorp as the fourth most admired utility in America.

UtiliCorp's world headquarters are located in this beautifully restored building at 20 West Ninth Street in Kansas City.

One of the keys to its success is a highly motivated workforce. At the end of 2000, about 85 percent of UtiliCorp's North American employees were shareholders in the company, together owning more than 13 percent of all shares outstanding. Many of those workers are based downtown at the company's world headquarters in one of Kansas City's architectural jewels, 20 West Ninth Street. UtiliCorp completed its award-winning restoration of the historic 10-story structure, the former New York Life Building, in 1996. Built in 1888, it is known as Kansas City's first skyscraper.

UtiliCorp's rapid growth to become an international energy and services company is the result of an aggressive strategy of regulated and non-regulated energy acquisitions and investments. In North America, the company distributes energy through networks of wires and pipes to 408,000 electric customers in Missouri, Kansas, and Colorado and 863,000 natural gas customers in seven states—Missouri, Kansas, Colorado, Nebraska, Iowa, Michigan, and Minnesota. UtiliCorp markets in all of those states under the EnergyOne® brand through seven divisions, including Missouri Public Service and St. Joseph Light & Power in northwest Missouri, and Kansas Public Service in the Lawrence, Kansas area.

The main lobby of 20 West Ninth Street features a barrel-vaulted ceiling and Italian mosaic tile floors.

Sources of electricity UtiliCorp delivers to customers in Kansas and Missouri include two wind power projects.

UtiliCorp Networks Canada serves more than 500,000 electric customers in British Columbia and Alberta.

Through various ownership positions in network operations in Australasia, UtiliCorp serves more than 600,000 electric and gas customers in New Zealand and about 1.6 million in Australia. In both countries, the company is also active in the development and operation of broadband fiber-optic networks.

UtiliCorp launched broadband telecommunications services in late 2000 in parts of the Greater Kansas City area. It also owns about 35 percent of Houston-based Quanta Services, which builds and maintains lines for cable TV and telecommunications companies as well as for gas and electric utilities.

Company Heritage

UtiliCorp's roots date back to Lemuel Green who operated a water-turned generator in the small Kansas town of Alton. In 1908, Lemuel Green began selling excess power to anyone who would purchase it. After milling flour for a number of years, Green quit milling and began stringing power lines across Western Kansas. In 1918, he built a generator near Pleasant Hill, Missouri, and started what became known as Missouri Public Service Co.

Green's two great-grandsons guide UtiliCorp's growth and further transformation today. Richard C. Green, Jr., 46, has been chairman of the board since 1989 and was chief executive officer for 17 years. He joined the company in 1976, held various positions, and launched the company's growth strategy in 1985 when UtiliCorp United was formed from Missouri Public Service Company.

Robert K. Green, 39, has served as the company's president since 1996 and succeeded his brother as CEO in 2002. He is also CEO of the Aquila, Inc., subsidiary.

"UtiliCorp formulated a disciplined strategic plan designed to expand the company's products, multiply its markets and diversify its risks, without straying from its core expertise in energy," says Rick Green. "The first step was to expand the company into other states to diversify the risk—regulatory, environmental, geographic, and demographic. Then, as foreign markets opened up UtiliCorp searched abroad for undervalued, often newly privatized, properties."

Robert Green says "value" is the underlying aspect of UtiliCorp's business strategy.

"It all goes back to delivering good value and good service to the customer. With that philosophy in mind, the company is expanding into new markets one step at a time making sure to add value with each step," he said. "Five years from now I would like us to be in 10 new markets and recognized as the premiere network operator and energy merchant in all of our markets. And above all, I'd like to be creating tremendous shareholder value." 🏵

Acquiring an electric utility in Alberta in 2000 expanded UtiliCorp's presence in Canada, where it now has 500,000 customers.

Aquila, Inc.

With a name that is Latin for eagle, it is no wonder that Aquila, Inc., an energy trader on two continents, as well as a global marketer of energy and associated risk management products and services, soars among its competitors. Aquila trades and bundles capital, weather-related, and actual risk-management products around energy commodities to manage the total risk profile of clients.

Natural gas pipelines and storage facilities play a role in Aquila's wholesale energy business.

Those clients, largely utilities and industrial firms, don't like to see the cost of their energy going up and down like a yo-yo, since energy is a major expense for them and can easily destroy earnings growth. That's where having a partner like Aquila adds a lot of value. The company uses its knowledge of energy and related markets to help clients grow their businesses smoothly year after year. In managing its clients' energy risk, Aquila completes some 50,000 transactions a month, nearly $80,000 worth of business every minute, every day of the year. Total 12-month sales from Aquila's businesses reached $39.3 billion in September 2001.

More specifically, the company trades natural gas, electricity, coal, crude oil, petroleum products, weather derivatives, and bandwidth. Aquila leverages this multi-commodity expertise to provide physical delivery, risk management, asset optimization, and consulting services to the global market.

Aquila was 20 percent owned by the public for most of 2001, but now is again wholly owned by UtiliCorp United. Both companies are headquartered in downtown Kansas City. UtiliCorp is an international energy company with more than 4 million customers in the U.S., Canada, the United Kingdom, New Zealand, and Australia.

UtiliCorp started Aquila Energy in the mid-1980s when deregulation of the natural gas industry began. The company was originally formed to trade and market wholesale natural gas. In the mid-1990s, wholesale power was deregulated, and Aquila added electricity to its list of traded commodities. Then in quick order Aquila began developing a long list of specially designed risk management products, including many firsts for the industry. When Aquila first opened its doors it had only two employees. Now it has more than 1,100, and competes with well-known industry giants like Duke, Dynegy, and Enron. Yet, it owns relatively few assets compared to those companies. Aquila's strategy has been to develop its expertise and products and then acquire a few key assets that support those strategically. For example, in December 2000, Aquila paid $225 million to acquire the six domestic power plants of New Jersey-based GPU International. Combined with its interests in other facilities owned or under development, Aquila controls nearly 4,100 megawatts of electric generation.

In its home state, Aquila recently built the $277 million Aries power plant near Kansas City, in Pleasant Hill, Missouri. At the beginning of the summer of 2001, the plant began producing power. The Aries plant is fueled by natural gas, and its air and water emissions are among the lowest in the industry. UtiliCorp's Missouri Public Service division will receive a major share of its electricity output, and Aquila will sell the rest of the output to other companies.

Aquila owns assets other than power plants. For example, near Huntington, West Virginia, it owns a full-service coal handling operation that produces revenues of around $5 million annually. The site has been profitable because it not only lies in an area of very high coal consumption, but also provides easy access to trucks, trains, and river barges.

Aquila's trading floor in Kansas City provides traders with sophisticated tools for keeping in touch with national and international markets.

In Texas, Aquila owns an underground storage complex west of Houston that can hold some 20 billion cubic feet of natural gas and has connections to 12 major pipeline systems. Having stored natural gas available for quick delivery is especially important to customers when there are unexpected temperature changes or other factors affecting demand for energy. Aquila also gathers, transports, and processes natural gas and natural gas liquids in Texas and Oklahoma.

Outside North America, the company wholesales natural gas and power in the United Kingdom, Norway, and Germany.

Robert Green, UtiliCorp's president and CEO and Aquila's chairman and CEO, says that Aquila provides structured products to remove volatility from a client's balance sheet and income statement.

Aquila has added significantly to its portfolio of power projects in the last two years, including this project in Georgia.

"We see tremendous demand from our client base for these services. Energy-intensive industries have been sensitized to the need for these products and services by the recent volatility in the energy markets, after many years of declining prices."

In 1996, Aquila created The GuaranteedWeather® family of products. The more than 30 different products minimize the risk of weather-related energy-price fluctuations. In the case of El Niño or some other major weather inhibitor, a utility company wants to hedge against seasonal temperature variations. The first step is to determine what part of the utility's total revenue is at risk and the exact effect of temperature variations on that percentage. After reading meteorological information, Aquila determines the probability for temperature variations and determines what options vary from normal by more than a predetermined percent.

Weather isn't the only volumetric risk Aquila manages. GuaranteedGeneration℠ helps to protect generators from high spot-market power prices when a generating facility unexpectedly fails. Aquila is also developing products that will assist areas such as ski resorts, theme parks, and agriculture against the perils of snow removal.

Aquila began trading bandwidth capacity in 2000. The company expects this to eventually be a major commodity and growth area as use of the Internet and other telecom applications continues to grow in coming years.

Aquila's most critical investment is in its people. Its core team of operators is cross-trained in a number of disciplines including energy traders, wholesalers, weather and math experts, engineers, and financial analysts. Many of these came to Kansas City in 1999 and 2000 as Aquila consolidated several offices, including its former Omaha headquarters and trading operation.

Today, appropriately enough, from the top floor of Town Pavilion, Aquila has a commanding, eagle-eye's view of

Teamwork by experts in many fields has enabled Aquila to become one of the leaders in its industry.

not just the surrounding metro area, but also wholesale energy markets around the world. 🔳

Williams

Over the past 90 years, Williams has quietly grown into a multibillion-dollar company, which connects businesses to energy, delivering innovative, reliable products and services.

Williams has been around since 1908, when two Williams brothers began a construction company. That business grew into the world's leading pipeline engineering and construction firm. Under the Williams Brothers name, the company went public in 1957 with a net worth of about $8 million.

Today, Williams produces $10.4 billion in revenues and employs nearly 14,000 worldwide.

Headquartered in Tulsa, Oklahoma, the Fortune 500 company has been recognized by Fortune Magazine as one of America's Most Admired Pipeline Companies. Williams Gas Pipeline is one of the world's leading natural gas transporter.

Serving at the heartbeat of the company, CEO Keith Bailey developed the core values and beliefs, which have guided the company and will continue to do so in the future. The underlying message in these core values is that helping out the community's, schools, and charitable causes goes hand in hand with corporate success.

Powering Solutions for Today's Business

Williams provides customers with a full range of traditional and leading-edge energy services. The company marketing and trading unit buys and sells energy products nationwide including natural gas and gas liquids, crude oil, and refined products and electricity to local distribution companies and large industrial and commercial consumers in North America.

The company's petroleum services unit transports liquids through a 21-state pipeline system, distributes products at 77 terminals, and produces and markets ethanol and its bio-products. The company owns and operates Alaska's largest refinery and Tennessee's only refinery.

Once petroleum products reach Kansas City they are distributed through Williams' Kansas City Fairfax district terminal into tank trucks that carry the gasoline and distillates to various Kansas City retail gasoline stations

Refined Petroleum Products Loading Rack Terminal at Kansas City, Kansas. *Photo by Todd Feeback, Plunge Productions*

Williams Gas Central Pumping Station at Ottawa, Kansas. *Photo by Todd Feeback, Plunge Productions*

and bulk plant customers. The Kansas City terminal pumps jet fuel to the Kansas City International Airport.

Williams serves as a common carrier pipeline company that owns its own lines and allows others, even competitors to ship product through the system.

Also operating in the Fairfax district at Williams is a Systems Laboratory that is used to ensure quality control of products by testing representative samples of each product. Williams provides testing for octane, gravity of the product, and color to pipeline companies who may need laboratory services.

In addition, Williams operates a liquefied petroleum gas pipeline in Kearney, Missouri, that provides propane to rural areas of the Midwest.

More than 48 million residential, industrial, and commercial natural gas users depend on Williams to deliver the energy they need. The natural gas pipeline network stretches from coast to coast with access to every major supply basin in the country. Together, the company's five natural gas pipelines are among the nation's largest-volume transports of natural gas, transporting approximately 18 percent of all the natural gas consumed.

Williams is the company that pipes nearly a billion cubic feet of natural gas to Kansas City on a cold winter day. The company's pipeline serves as a delivery vehicle for companies like Missouri Gas Energy, KCP&L, Kansas Gas Service, Greeley Gas, and Western Resources Inc.

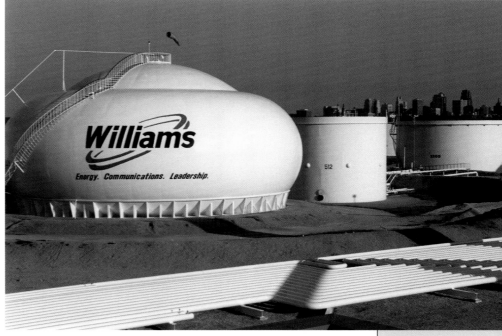

Kansas City Refined Tank Farm with Kansas City downtown in background. Photo by Todd Feeback, Plunge Productions

New Construction at Ottawa, Kansas. Photo by Todd Feeback, Plunge Productions

Community Involvement

Williams takes great pride in having achieved the United Way of America's Spirit Award with its record-breaking donations giving tens of millions of dollars annually in combined company and employee gifts annually.

Other projects Williams supports include adopt-a-school program, Junior Achievement, and the Nature Conservancy—just to name a few.

Locally, Williams has hosted two "After Hours" events for the Greater Kansas City Chamber of Commerce and continues to serve as a community-minded corporation with the Kansas City area. The company works aggressively with the Mining and Reclamation Council (MARC) and the chamber in Kansas City to help meet Kansas City's emissions standards.

"We have been a leader in our industry and it feels good to be associated with a company that continues to set leading-edge standards," said Book Lawrence, community affairs manager for Williams. "The most important aspect of Williams, however, is the people. The people associated with the company are supportive, encouraging, and provide opportunities for success."

Kansas City, Missouri Water Services

Water is one of the most important resources and primary needs in life. The Kansas City Water Services Department has been protecting and improving upon the quality of that need for more than 125 years.

From its untreated natural state in the Missouri River to a customer's faucet, water is treated and processed using the highest standards and most advanced techniques around.

Water Services pumps water from the Missouri River through its treatment plants for chemical treating and softening. From here it is distributed through the 2,300-mile network of water mains to 150,000 plus customers throughout the metro area. The department has a capacity to produce up to 240 million gallons of water per day (mgd), with an average day totaling approximately 140 mgd.

With all of these upgrades and continual expansions, Kansas City Water Services has managed to keep water rates some of the lowest in the metro area, as well as nationally.

Gurnie Gunter, director of Kansas City Water Services said water rates for residential and commercial users will not increase this year. "By holding the line on water rates we provide an outstanding value to our customers," Gunter said.

Seven water towers and 10 underground storage reservoirs dot the city ensuring adequate water pressure 24-hours-a-day.

He noted that the consistency of these water rates is partly a result of Water Services' sales of wholesale water to 30 plus surrounding cities and water districts. This has generated new revenue that has offset the increasing cost of supplying water to customers.

In addition to providing clean drinking water, Water Services also tackles drainage and flooding issues through the stormwater engineering division. Currently, this division is conducting comprehensive master plans that will look at the city's watersheds, floodplain management, design, construction, enlargement, replacement, and maintenance of the city's stormwater management facilities. The city's Water Services also has a wastewater division that focuses on the disposal and treatment of wastewater. This division has eight wastewater facilities that work 24 hours a day to treat and return wastewater back to nature. These facilities return resources to their natural state in better quality than when they were removed from the river.

Besides protecting the environment via wastewater treatment, Water Services also has an industrial waste division that assists businesses with pollution prevention by encouraging pretreatment of waste before it enters the system. The division also monitors the use of industrial waste to the keep the treatment plant at full efficiency and by tracking down polluters.

Kansas City has been divided into 35 watersheds—the area that drains into a creek, stream, or river. Watershed assessment and planning are underway to establish recommendations for improvements.

Constructed in 1928, the Water Treatment Plant delivers more than 115 million gallons of potable water daily to customers throughout the region. Through constant vigilance and adjustments of chemical applications to remove all unwanted substances from the water, we transform the "muddy Mo" to safe, clean drinking water.

With an ever-expanding customer base and growing need for cost-efficient drinking water in the area, Water Services is partnering with the City of Lee's Summit to build a pump station and water reservoir as part of the South Terminal Project. This joint effort is the first of its kind for Water Services.

In addition to expanding its water service, Kansas City has started a new bottled water distribution program. The bottled water is available at the Kansas City Zoo, Bartle Hall, and many outdoor recreational facilities in the metro area, as well as QuikTrip and other retail establishments.

Water Services also has an accredited, nationally recognized quality-control laboratory that analyzes more than 1,100 water and wastewater samples weekly for the city. That is over 60,000 analyses annually. This includes other water sources, industries, and consumers with wells. Technicians perform routine monitoring for more than 200 compounds.

Through all of the changes and expansions that Kansas City Water Services has undergone, the core focus of the department will always be the importance of serving one of its customers most basic needs: clean drinking water. The Kansas City Water Services has provided that for over a century, and will continue to do so well into the future.

Midway Ford Truck Center, Inc.

Midway Ford Truck Center is a 40-year-old company that specializes in satisfying commercial and fleet transportation needs. The employee-owned business is one of the largest and most respected truck dealerships in the world. Headquartered on more than 27-acres fronting I-435 just north of the Missouri River in northeast Kansas City, Missouri, Midway is a full-service dealer for Ford, Sterling, and Hino trucks. Midway also operates body shop and warehouse locations in Kansas City, Missouri, a parts and service branch in Kansas City, Kansas, and two out-of-area truck sales businesses. The 265 employee owners in the Kansas City area provide 24-hour parts and service support for Midway customers.

Midway became the first Ford dealership in the country to establish an Employee Stock Ownership Plan in 1982. Today, the ESOP is Midway's largest shareholder. Fifteen Midway managers own the balance of the stock. Employee ownership has worked extremely well for Midway and its customers. Employee owners with the authority to satisfy customer needs produce continuity of relationships, loyalty, and satisfaction exceeding expectations in this industry.

Midway's ownership mentality, coupled with adherence to the Golden Rule, have been the cornerstones for company growth and success. Midway is the first motor vehicle dealership to be recognized by the Kansas City Chamber of Commerce as one of its "Top 10 Small Businesses." The dealership repeatedly receives awards from Ford as one of its best dealerships measured by customer satisfaction, including Ford's Chairman's and President's Awards.

Strong support for the community is something Midway employees do naturally. Many team members participate as Scout Leaders for the Boy Scouts of America, serve as coaches in sporting activities, and work with area schools on apprenticeship programs to provide needed mentors. In addition, Midway sponsors various fund-raising events throughout the year for Children's Mercy Hospital, as well as the United Way and Ford-related charities.

Beginning its second 40 years, Midway is well positioned for the future. Midway expects to leverage its technological superiority to enhance customer service and value. The current Web site (*www.midwaytrucks.com*) offers a complete listing of inventory information as well as serving as an e-commerce site for fleet customers.

Recognizing the need for leadership and continuity, Midway is grooming successors so that its third generation of top management will continue the strong leadership of their predecessors. Midway employee owners will continue Midway's primary purpose of "serving customers so well that they remain loyal to Midway."

Company President Gary McClung and Chairman Don Ahnger are proud of their Midway ESOP partners and the many success stories that they produce. Customer satisfaction with Midway's sales and service operations, as evaluated by Ford Motor Company's voice of the customer surveys, continues to improve. Midway parts and service departments continue to grow, establishing new records nearly every month.

"I am very confident that Midway Ford Truck Center will continue its leadership position in Kansas City," said Don Ahnger. "Our outstanding people and the quality products and services we sell will serve Kansas City area transportation needs well."

Midway Ford Truck Center offers trucks of all sizes, as well as parts, service, body repair, and twenty-four hour support.

Enterprise Index

HDR, Inc.
4435 Main Street, Suite 1000
Kansas City, Missouri 64115
Phone: (816)360-2725
Fax: (816)360-2777
E-mail: vmullen@hdrinc.com
www.hdrinc.com
Pages 172-173

Helzberg Diamonds
1825 Swift Avenue
North Kansas City, Missouri 64116
Phone: (800)669-7780
www.helzberg.com
Pages 224-225

Historic Suites of America
612 Central
Kansas City, Missouri 64105
Phone: (816)842-6544
Fax: (816)842-0656
Pages 226-227

HNTB Architects Engineers Planners
715 Kirk Drive
Kansas City, Missouri 64105
Phone: (816)472-1201
Fax: (816)472-4060
www.hntb.com
Page 177

Honeywell Federal Manufacturing & Technologies
2000 East 95th Street
Post Office Box 419159
Kansas City, Missouri 64141-6159
Phone: (816)997-2000
Fax: (816)997-3331
www.kcp.com
Pages 214-215

J.E. Dunn Construction
929 Holmes
Kansas City, Missouri 64106-2682
Phone: (816)474-8600
Fax: (816)460-2769
E-mail: info@jedunn.com
www.jedunn.com
Pages 234-235

James B. Nutter & Company
4153 Broadway
Kansas City, Missouri 64111
Phone: (816)531-2345
Fax: (816)756-2349
www.jamesbnutter.com
Pages 238-239

John Deere
11145 Thompson Avenue
Lenexa, Kansas 66219
Phone: (913)310-8324
Fax: (913)310-8394
www.johndeere.com
Pages 216-217

Johnson County Community College
12345 College Boulevard
Overland Park, Kansas 66210
Phone: (913)469-8500
Fax: (913)469-4409
www.jccc.net
Page 188

Kansas City, Missouri Water Services
414 East 12th Street
5th Floor, City Hall
Kansas City, Missouri 64106
Phone: (816)513-2171
E-mail: water@kcmo.org
www.kcmo.org
Pages 254-255

Kansas City Power & Light
Post Office Box 418679
Kansas City, Missouri 64141-9679
Phone: (816)556-2069
Fax: (816)556-2222
E-mail: bill.ackerly@kcpl.com
www.kcpl.com
Pages 212-213

KPMG LLP
1000 Walnut, Suite 1600
Kansas City, Missouri 64106
Phone: (816)474-6480
Fax: (816)556-9711
www.kpmg.com
Pages 158-159

KU Med
3901 Rainbow Boulevard
Kansas City, Kansas 66160
Phone: (913)588-1227
Fax: (913)588-5785
www.kumed.com
Page 204

La Petite Academy, Inc.
14 Corporate Woods
8717 West 110th Street #300
Overland Park, Kansas 66210
Phone: (913)345-1250
Fax: (913)345-0836
www.lapetite.com
Page 189

Lathrop & Gage
2345 Grand Boulevard
Suite 2800
Kansas City, Missouri 64108
Phone: (816)292-2000
Fax: (816)292-2001
E-mail: pbesheer@lathropgage.com
www.lathropgage.com
Pages 162-163

Mid America Health
8320 Ward Parkway
Kansas City, Missouri 64114-2027
Phone: (816)221-8400
Fax: (816)221-1870
www.midamericahealth.com
Pages 200-201

Midway Ford Truck Center, Inc.
7601 Northeast 38th Street
Kansas City, Missouri 64161
Phone: (816)455-3000
Fax: (816)455-0578
www.midwaytrucks.com
Page 256

Polsinelli Shalton & Welte
700 West 47th Street, Suite 1000
Kansas City, Missouri 64112
Phone: (816)753-1000
Fax: (816)753-1536
E-mail: pswlaw@pswlaw.com
www.pswlaw.com
Pages 168-169

The Quarterage Hotel
560 Westport Road
Kansas City, Missouri 64111
Phone: (816)931-0001
Fax: (816)931-8891
E-mail: info@quarteragehotel.com
www.quarteragehotel.com
Page 229

Rockhurst University
1100 Rockhurst Road
Kansas City, Missouri 64110
Phone: (800)842-6776
Fax: (816)501-4241
E-mail: admission@rockhurst.edu
www.rockhurst.edu
Pages 184-185

Saint Luke's—Shawnee Mission Health System
10920 Elm Avenue
Kansas City, Missouri 64134
Phone: (816)932-6220
E-mail: info@saint-lukes.org
www.saint-lukes.org
Pages 194-197

Samuel U. Rodgers Community Health Center
825 Euclid Avenue
Kansas City, Missouri 64128
Phone: (816)474-4920
Fax: (816)474-6475
E-mail: ivoncollins@samuel-rodgers.org
Page 205

Enterprise Index

Sheet Metal and Air Conditioning Contractors National Association—Kansas City (SMACNA-KC)
777 Admiral Boulevard
Kansas City, Missouri 64106
Phone: (816)421-3360
Fax: (816)421-3362
E-mail: khensa@smacnakc.com
 information@smacnakc.com
www.smacnakc.com
Pages 240-241

Sheet Metal Workers Local Union No. 2
2902 Blue Ridge Boulevard
Kansas City, Missouri 64129
Phone: (816)254-8021
Fax: (816)254-0018
E-mail: bob@sheetmetal2.org
Page 244

State Street
801 Pennsylvania
Kansas City, Missouri 64105
Phone: (816)871-9328
Fax: (816)871-9627
E-mail: dlholland@statestreetkc.com
www.statestreetkc.com
Pages 156-157

Stowers Institute for Medical Research
1000 East 50th Street
Kansas City, Missouri 64110
Phone: (816)926-4000
Fax: (816)444-8644
E-mail: info@stowers-institute.org
www.stowers-institute.org
Page 155

Transamerica Occidental Life Insurance Company
1100 Walnut, Suite 2400
Kansas City, Missouri 64106
Phone: (816)855-5000
Fax: (816)855-5230
Pages 170-171

The University of Health Sciences
1750 East Independence Avenue
Kansas City, Missouri 64106
Phone: (816)283-2300
Fax: (816)283-2303
E-mail: k.pletz@uhs.edu
www.uhs.edu
Pages 180-183

The University of Kansas
1314 Jayhawk Boulevard
Lawrence, Kansas 66045-3175
Phone: (785)864-3256
Fax: (785)864-3339
E-mail: kurelations@ku.edu
www.ku.edu
Page 190

University of Missouri-Kansas City
5100 Rockhill Road
Kansas City, Missouri 64110-2499
Phone: (816)235-1000
Fax: (816)235-5189
E-mail: admit@umkc.edu
www.umkc.edu
Page 191

UtiliCorp United
20 West Ninth Street
Kansas City, Missouri 64105
Phone: (816)421-6600
Fax: (816)467-3005
www.utilicorp.com
Pages 248-249

Williams
13424 West 98th Street
Shawnee Mission, Kansas 66215
Phone: (913)310-7700
Fax: (913)310-7790
E-mail: book.lawrence@williams.com
www.williams.com
Pages 252-253

Yellow Corporation
10990 Roe Avenue
Overland Park, Kansas 66211
Phone: (913)344-3000
www.yellowcorp.com
Pages 210-211